TOEFL iBT®
VOCABULARY

. . . .

FLASH REVIEW

TOEFL iBT®
VOCABULARY

LEARNINGEXPRESS®

NEW YORK

Copyright © 2014 Learning Express, LLC.
All rights reserved under International and Pan
American Copyright Conventions. Published in the
United States by LearningExpress, LLC, New York.

Cataloging-in-Publication Data is on file with the
Library of Congress.

Printed in the United States of America

9 8 7 6 5 4 3 2 1

First Edition

ISBN 978-1-57685-958-2

For more information or to place an order, contact
LearningExpress at:
    80 Broad Street
    Suite 400
    New York, NY 10004

CONTENTS

INTRODUCTION............................... 1

A 7

B 61

C 81

D 115

E 145

F 179

G 195

H 205

I 213

J 247

L 251

M 259

N 281

O 289

P 305

Q 353

R 359

S 381

T 417

U 435

V 441

W 453

X 455

Z 457

INTRODUCTION

About the TOEFL iBT® Exam

The TOEFL iBT® is an Internet-based exam (taken on a standard QWERTY computer keyboard) that is designed to test your English knowledge and skill at the university level. If you're eager to study in an English-speaking country, you should plan to take this test—and careful practice and preparation is essential for success on test day.

The TOEFL iBT® gauges your ability to communicate and perform in an academic setting through effective listening, reading, writing, and speaking. These skills are important to have for success in the classroom—to follow and participate in class discussions, complete assignments, deliver presentations, keep up with coursework, and more.

Millions of prospective students from around the world take the test each year, prior to studying in English-speaking academic environments, in order to demonstrate proficiency in English, and to satisfy requirements for visas or admission to their chosen education programs.

Information regarding registration, fees, test dates, what to expect on test day, and more can be obtained from the official Educational Testing Service website.

The TOEFL iBT® exam is approximately 4½ hours long, which includes a mandatory 10-minute break midway through the test. It consists of the following four sections:

- **Reading:** Includes three or four reading passages and approximately 36–56 questions based on the reading. You'll have 60–80 minutes to complete this section.
- **Listening:** Includes lectures, classroom discussions, and conversations that you are asked to listen to, and approximately 34-51 questions that are designed to test your understanding of what you listened to. You'll have 60–90 minutes to complete this section. English

accents for test content in this section will vary.

- **Speaking:** Includes six tasks that ask you to express an opinion on a provided topic, and speak about reading and listening tasks. You'll have 20 minutes to complete this section. English accents for test content in this section will vary.
- **Writing:** Includes two tasks that ask you to write essay responses/support an opinion based on reading and listening tasks.

Please note that the test may also include additional unscored Reading or Listening section questions, which are solely used by ETS and will not count toward your test score.

How the TOEFL iBT® Exam is Scored

Your score on the TOEFL iBT® exam is determined by your responses to the questions and tasks provided. For each of the four sections of the exam, you'll receive a scaled score between 0–30. Your score is determined by a mix of human and automated scoring, designed to accurately assess your abilities. Your total test score will be the sum of your four scaled section scores, and will range between 0–120.

Your score also includes feedback regarding your test performance, which reflects your English-language skill level in the areas tested. In addition, your score will be valid for two years after the test date, and you can retake the test as many times as you'd like.

In order to receive a score on the exam, you must write at least one essay in the Writing section; complete at least one Speaking section task; and answer at least one question in each of the Reading and Listening sections. For additional test information, please visit the official ETS website.

How to Use this Book

TOEFL iBT® Vocabulary Flash Review is designed to help you prepare for and succeed on the official exam. A strong vocabulary is essential—both for success on this exam and for success in an English-speaking academic program. It contains more than 600 of the most commonly covered vocabulary words on the exam, along with their parts of speech, pronunciations, definitions, and sample sentences, for quick and effective study and review. The terms are alphabetized for easy access.

TOEFL iBT® Vocabulary Flash Review works well as a stand-alone study tool, but it is recommended that it be used to supplement additional preparation for the exam. The following are some suggestions for making the most of this effective resource as you structure your study plan:

- Do not try to learn or memorize all of the more than 600 words covered in this book all at once. The best approach is to build a realistic study schedule that lets you review 10–15 words per day, and then quiz yourself to see how well you've learned them.
- Mark the words that you have trouble with, so that they will be easy to return to later for further study.
- Make the most of this book's portability—take it with you for studying on car trips, between classes, while commuting, or whenever you have free time.

- Visit the official ETS website for additional information to help you be prepared on test day.

Best of luck on the exam—and in achieving your goals!

A

ABATE
(ă·'bayt) v.

. . . .

ABERRATION
(ă b·ĕ·'ray·shŏn) n.

. . . .

ABEYANCE
(ă·'bay·ă ns) n.

to lessen in strength, intensity, or degree; to subside.

As the violent storm abated, we began to survey the damage it caused.

. . . .

deviation from what is normal, distortion.

His new scientific theory was deemed an aberration by his very conservative colleagues.

. . . .

suspension, being temporarily suspended or set aside.

Construction of the highway is in abeyance until we get agency approval.

ABHOR
(ab·'hohr) v.

. . . .

ABJURE
(ab·'joor) v.

. . . .

ABROGATE
('ab·rŏ·gayt) v.

A

to regard with horror or repugnance; to detest.

I know Carlos abhors politics, but he should still get out and vote.

. . . .

1. to repudiate or renounce under oath.
2. to give up or reject.

When Joseph became a citizen, he had to abjure his allegiance to his country of origin.

. . . .

to abolish, do away with, formally revoke.

The dictator abrogated agreements that no longer suited his purposes.

ABSCOND
(ab·'skond) v.

. . . .

ABSOLUTION
(ab·sŏ·'loo·shŏn) n.

. . . .

ABSTAIN
(ab·'stayn) v.

to go away secretly and hide oneself, especially after wrongdoing to avoid prosecution.

He threw down his gun and absconded from the scene of the crime.

. . . .

1. to absolve or clear of blame or guilt.
2. a formal declaration of forgiveness, redemption.

The jury granted Alan the absolution he deserved.

. . . .

1. to choose to refrain from an action or practice.
2. to refrain from voting.

I have decided to abstain on this issue.

ABSTEMIOUS
(ab·'stee·mee·ŭs) adj.

. . . .

ABSTRUSE
(ab·'stroos) adj.

. . . .

ABYSMAL
(ă·'biz·măl) adj.

A

1. using or consuming sparingly; used with temperance or restraint.
2. eating and drinking in moderation; sparing in the indulgence of appetites or passions.

After Vadeem gained 30 pounds, he decided he needed a more abstemious diet.

• •

difficult to comprehend; obscure.

Albert Einstein's abstruse calculations can be understood by only a few people.

• •

1. extreme, limitless, profound.
2. extremely bad.

It was not surprising that the movie was a flop, as the reviews were abysmal.

ACCOLADE
('ak·ŏ·layd) n.

. . . .

ACCRETION
(ă·'kree·shŏn) n.

. . . .

ACQUIESCE
(ak·wee·'es) v.

1. praise or approval.   [most common]
2. a ceremonial embrace in greeting.
3. a ceremonious tap on the shoulder with a sword to mark the conferring of knighthood.

He received accolades from his superiors for finding ways to cut costs and increase productivity.

. . . .

1. growth or increase by gradual, successive addition; building up.
2. (in biology) the growing together of parts that are normally separate.

The accretion of sediment in the harbor channel caused boats to run aground.

. . . .

to comply, give in, or consent without protest.

After the police officer explained why the street was closed to pedestrian traffic, I acquiesced and walked to the next street.

ACRID
('ak·rĭd) adj.

. . . .

ACRIMONIOUS
(ak·rĭ·'moh·nee·ŭs) adj.

. . . .

ACUMEN
(ă·'kyoo·měn) n.

A

1. having an unpleasantly bitter, sharp taste or smell.
2. bitter or caustic in language or manner.

The burning tires in the junkyard gave off an acrid odor.

. . . .

bitter and sharp in language or tone.

Jasleen did not like her new neighbors; it was obvious in the acrimonious way she spoke to them.

. . . .

quickness, keenness, and accuracy of perception, judgment, or insight.

With Jonelle's acumen, she would make an excellent trial lawyer.

AD HOC
(ad 'hok) adj.

. . . .

ADAMANT
('ad·ă·mănt) adj.

. . . .

ADDLE
('ad·ĕl) v.

A

for a specific, often temporary, purpose; for this case only.

An ad hoc committee will be formed to investigate Stella's allegations.

. . . .

1. unyielding to requests or appeals.
2. firm, inflexible.

The senator was adamant that no changes would be made to the defense budget.

. . . .

1. to muddle or confuse.
2. to become rotten, as in an egg.

The prosecuting attorney's questions addled the defendant.

ADO
(ă·'doo) n.

. . . .

ADROIT
(ă·'droit) adj.

. . . .

AGRARIAN
(ă·'grair·ee·ăn) adj.

fuss, trouble, bother.

Without much ado, she completed her book report.

. . . .

skillful, clever, or adept in action or in thought; dexterous, deft.

Priya is a very adroit seamstress; she should have your trousers fixed in no time.

. . . .

relating to or concerning land and its ownership or cultivation.

Although his family tried to convince him to move to a big city, Greg preferred his agrarian life as a farmer.

AFICIONADO
(ă·fish·yo·'nah·doh) n.

. . . .

ALACRITY
(ă·'lak·ri·tee) n.

. . . .

ALLAY
(ă·'lay) v.

a fan or devotee, especially of a sport or pastime.

Sal is such a Rolling Stones aficionado that he bought tickets to all ten Giants Stadium concerts.

· ·

a cheerful willingness; being happily ready and eager.

The alacrity she brought to her job helped her move up the corporate ladder quickly.

· ·

1. to reduce the intensity of; to alleviate.
2. to calm, put to rest.

The remarks by the CEO did not allay the concerns of the employees.

ALLUDE
(ă·'lood) v.

. . . .

ALTERCATION
(awl·tĕr·'kay·shŏn) n.

. . . .

AMIABLE
('ay·mee·ă·bĕl) adj.

A

to make an indirect reference to.

The presidential candidate alluded to the recent unemployment problem by saying, "We've all made sacrifices."

. . . .

a heated dispute or quarrel.

To prevent an altercation at social functions, one should avoid discussing politics and religion.

. . . .

friendly and agreeable; good natured, likable, pleasing.

Miguel was usually the first person invited to a party, as his amiable personality drew people to him.

AMITY
('am·ĭ·tee) n.

. . . .

AMBIVALENT
(am·'biv·ă·lĕnt) adj.

. . . .

AMELIORATE
(ă·'meel·yŏ·rayt) v.

friendship; a state of friendly or peaceful relations.

Amity had existed between Denise and Suzanne once they decided not to fight about money.

. . . .

having mixed or conflicting feelings about a person, thing, or situation; uncertain.

She was ambivalent about the proposal for the shopping center, because she understood both the arguments for and against its construction.

. . . .

to make or become better, to improve.

The diplomat was able to ameliorate the tense situation between the two nations.

AMORPHOUS
(ă·'mor·fŭs) adj.

· ·

AMULET
('am·yŭ·lit) n.

· ·

ANACHRONISM
(ă·'nak·rŏ·niz·ĕm) n.

A

1. having no definite form or distinct shape; shapeless.
2. of no particular kind or character, anomalous.

Andrea looked up at the amorphous clouds in the sky.

· ·

something worn around the neck as a charm against evil.

The princess wore an amulet after being cursed by a wizard.

· ·

1. something that is placed into an incorrect historical period.
2. a person, custom, or idea that is out of date.

With the rise in popularity of cell phones, pagers seem like an anachronism.

ANARCHY
('an·ă r·kee) n.

. . . .

ANOMALY
(ă·'nom·ă·lee) n.

. . . .

ANTAGONIST
(an·'tag·ŏ·nist) n.

A

1. the complete absence of government or control resulting in lawlessness.
2. political disorder and confusion.

After the king's assassination, the country fell into a state of anarchy.

. . . .

something that deviates from the general rule or usual form; one that is irregular, peculiar, or abnormal.

Everyone in my family enjoys seafood, so my uncle's distaste for salmon is an anomaly.

. . . .

one who opposes or contends with another; an adversary, opponent.

Hillary was Mike's antagonist as they both competed for the lead role in the play.

ANTECEDENT
(an·ti·'see·dnt) n.

. . . .

ANTHROPOMORPHIC
(an·thrŏ·pŏ·'mor·fik) adj.

. . . .

ANTIPATHY
(an·'tip·ă·thee) n.

TOEFL iBT® VOCABULARY FLASH REVIEW

that which precedes; the thing, circumstance, or event that came before.

The police are trying to determine the antecedent to the deadly car crash.

· ·

attributing human characteristics, motivations, or behavior to animals or inanimate objects.

Many mythologies are about anthropomorphic deities, who express human characteristics such as love, envy, and sadness.

· ·

1. a strong aversion or dislike.
2. an object of aversion.

Peter felt antipathy for his classmate after he stole his wallet.

ANTITHESIS
(an·'tith·ĕ·sis) n.

. . . .

APATHETIC
(ap·ă·'thet·ik) adj.

. . . .

APERTURE
('ap·ĕr·chŭr) n.

the direct or exact opposite, opposition or
contrast.

*Martin's parenting style is the antithesis of
mine: He is strict, I am not.*

• •

feeling or showing a lack of interest, concern,
or emotion; indifferent, unresponsive.

*Many students were apathetic when the
principal resigned after 30 years.*

• •

an opening or gap, especially one that lets in
light.

*The aperture setting on a camera has to be set
perfectly to ensure that pictures have enough
light.*

APEX
('ay·peks) n.

. . . .

APOCALYPSE
(ă·'pok·ă·lips) n.

. . . .

APOSTATE
(ă·'pos·tayt) n.

A

1. the highest point.
2. tip, pointed end.

Upon reaching the apex of the mountain, the climbers placed their flag in the snow.

· ·

a cataclysmic event bringing about total devastation or the end of the world.

Many people feared an apocalypse immediately following the development of nuclear weapons.

· ·

one who abandons long-held religious or political convictions.

Reverend Gift lost his faith and left the ministry, not caring if he'd be seen as an apostate by colleagues.

APOTHEOSIS
(ă·poth·ee·'oh·sis) n.

. . . .

APPEASE
(ă·'peez) v.

. . . .

APPRAISE
(ă·'prayz) v.

A

deification, an exalted or glorified ideal.

Hanson was so in love with Marge that to him she was an apotheosis.

· ·

to make calm or quiet, soothe; to still or pacify.

The only way to appease Lawrence is to concede that he is right.

· ·

1. to evaluate.
2. to establish value or estimate the worth of.

The art dealer appraised the value of the painting.

APPRISE
(ă·'prīz) v.

. . . .

APPROBATION
(ap·rŏ·'bay·shŏn) n.

. . . .

APPROPRIATE
(ă·'prŏ·prĕ·īt) adj.

to give notice or information to; to make aware of, inform.

The teacher apprised the class as to when the midterm and final exams would occur.

. . . .

approval.

The local authorities issued an approbation to close the street for a festival on St. Patrick's Day.

. . . .

suitable for a particular person, condition, occasion, or place; fitting.

(ă·'proh·pree·ayt) *v.* to take for one's own use, often without permission; to set aside for a special purpose.

The state legislature will appropriate $2 million from the annual budget to build a new bridge on the interstate highway.

APROPOS
(ap·rŏ'poh) adj.

. . . .

ARCANE
(ahr·'kayn) adj.

. . . .

ARCHAIC
(ahr·'kay·ik) adj.

A

appropriate to the situation; suitable to what is being said or done.

adv. 1. by the way, incidentally.
    2. at an appropriate or opportune time.

Chancey's comments may have been disturbing, but they were definitely apropos.

. . . .

mysterious, secret, beyond comprehension.

A number of college students in the 1980s became involved in the arcane game "Dungeons and Dragons."

. . . .

belonging to former or ancient times; characteristic of the past.

The archaic language of Chaucer's tales makes them difficult for many students to understand.

ARCHETYPE
('ahr·ki·tīp) n.

. . . .

ARDOR
('ahr·dŏr) n.

. . . .

ARDUOUS
('ahr·joo·ŭs) adj.

A

an original model from which others are copied; original pattern or prototype.

Elvis Presley served as the archetype for rock and roll performers in the 1950s.

. . . .

fiery intensity of feeling; passionate enthusiasm or zeal.

The ardor Larry brought to the campaign made him a natural spokesperson.

. . . .

1. very difficult, laborious; requiring great effort.
2. difficult to traverse or surmount.

Commander Shackleton's arduous journey through the Antarctic has become the subject of many books and movies.

ASCENT
(ă·'sent) n.

. . . .

ASCETIC
(ă·'set·ik) adj.

. . . .

ASKEW
(ă·'skyoo) adj. & adv.

A

1. an upward slope.
2. a movement upward, an advancement.

The rock climbers made the ascent up the side of the mountain.

. . . .

practicing self-denial, not allowing oneself pleasures or luxuries; austere.

Some religions require their leaders to lead an ascetic lifestyle as an example to their followers.

. . . .

crooked, not straight or level; to one side.

The pictures on the wall hung askew after my five-year-old son's birthday party.

ASPERITY
(ă·'sper·i·tee) n.

. . . .

ASSAY
(ă·'say) v.

. . . .

ASSENT
(ă·'sent) n.

A

TOEFL iBT® VOCABULARY FLASH REVIEW

harshness, severity; roughness of manner, ill temper, irritability.

The asperity that grumpy accountant Marvin brought to the meetings usually resulted in early adjournment.

. . . .

1. to try, put to a test.
2. to examine.
3. to judge critically, evaluate after an analysis.

The chief engineer wants a laboratory to assay the steel before using it in the construction project.

. . . .

agreement; concurrence; consent.

v. to agree to something, especially after thoughtful consideration.

In order to pass the new law, the committee must reach an assent.

ASSIDUOUS
(ă·'sij·oo·ŭs) adj.

. . . .

ASSUAGE
(ă·'swayj) v.

. . . .

ATTENUATE
(ă·'ten·yoo·ayt) v.

diligent, hardworking; persevering, unremitting.

Omar's teachers applaud his assiduous study habits.

· ·

to make something less severe, to soothe; to satisfy hunger or thirst.

The small cups of water offered to the marathon runners helped assuage their thirst.

· ·

1. to make thin or slender.
2. to weaken; to reduce in force, value, or degree.

The Russian army was able to attenuate the strength and number of the German forces by leading them inland during winter.

AUDACIOUS
(aw·'day·sh ŭs) adj.

. . . .

AUGMENT
(awg·'ment) v.

. . . .

AUGUST
(aw·'gust) adj.

fearlessly or recklessly daring or bold; unrestrained by convention or propriety.

Detective Malloy's methods were considered audacious by his superiors, but they often achieved good results.

• •

to increase in size, strength, or intensity; enlarge.

Arty tried to help Ann and Stan settle their differences, but his interference only augmented the problem.

• •

majestic, venerable; inspiring admiration or reverence.

Jackie Kennedy's august dignity in the days following her husband's assassination set a tone for the rest of the nation as it mourned.

AUSPICE
('aw·spis) n.

. . . .

AUSTERE
(aw·'steer) adj.

. . . .

AUTHORITARIAN
(ă·thor·i·'tair·i·ăn) adj.

A

1. protection or support, patronage.
2. a forecast or omen.

The children's art museum was able to continue operating through the auspices of an anonymous wealthy benefactor.

. . . .

1. severe or stern in attitude or appearance.
2. simple, unadorned, very plain.

I know my dad seems austere, but he's really very friendly.

. . . .

favoring complete, unquestioning obedience to authority, as opposed to individual freedom.

The military maintains an authoritarian environment for both its officers and enlisted men.

TOEFL iBT® VOCABULARY FLASH REVIEW

AUTOMATON
(aw·'tom·ă·tŏn) n.

. . . .

AUTONOMY
(aw·'ton·ŏ·mee) n.

. . . .

AVANT-GARDE
(a·vahnt·'gahrd) adj.

1. someone who acts or responds in a mechanical or robotic way.
2. a self-operating or automatic machine, a robot.

Each morning like an automaton, Natasha made coffee, cooked breakfast, and prepared her children's lunch.

. . . .

personal or political independence; self-government, self-determination.

The teenager desired a sense of autonomy and fewer rules from her parents.

. . . .

using or favoring an ultramodern or experimental style; innovative, cutting-edge, especially in the arts or literature.

Yvette prefers the avant-garde style of writers like Donald Barthelme to the traditional narrative technique.

AVERSION
(ă·'vur·zhŏn) n.

· ·

A

1. a strong, intense dislike; repugnance.
2. the object of this feeling.

Todd has an aversion to arugula and picks it out of his salads.

B

BALEFUL
('bayl·fŭl) adj.

. . . .

BALK
(bawk) v.

. . . .

BANAL
(bă·'nal) adj.

harmful, menacing, destructive, sinister.

Whether it's a man, woman, car, or animal, you can be certain to find at least one baleful character in a Stephen King horror novel.

. . . .

1. to stop abruptly and refuse to go on.
2. to obstinately refuse or oppose.

Jones was ready to capitulate and sell his land to the timber company, but he balked when he saw he would only be compensated for half of the value of his property.

. . . .

commonplace, trite; obvious and uninteresting.

I was expecting something original and exciting, but the film had a banal storyline and mediocre acting.

BANE
(bayn) n.

. . . .

BEGUILE
(bi·'gīl) v.

. . . .

BELIE
(bi·'lī) v.

1. cause of trouble, misery, distress, or harm.
2. poison.

The bane of the oak tree is the Asian beetle.

• •

to deceive or cheat through cunning; to distract the attention of, divert; to pass time in a pleasant manner, to amuse or charm.

Violet was able to beguile the spy, causing him to miss his secret meeting.

• •

1. to give a false impression, misrepresent.
2. to show to be false, to contradict.

By wearing an expensive suit and watch, Alan hoped to belie his lack of success to everyone at the reunion.

BELLICOSE
('bel·ĭ·kohs) adj.

. . . .

BELLIGERENT
(bi·'lij·ĕr·ĕnt) adj.

. . . .

BENEVOLENCE
(bĕ·'nev·ŏ·lĕns) n.

belligerent, quarrelsome, eager to make war.

The candidate was known for his bellicose nature, so there was little hope for peace following his election.

· ·

hostile and aggressive, showing an eagerness to fight.

Because Omar had a reputation for being belligerent, many people refused to associate with him.

· ·

the inclination to be kind and generous; a disposition to act charitably.

Regina showed benevolence when she volunteered to help raise money for the local soup kitchen.

BENIGN
(bi·'nīn) adj.

. . . .

BEVY
('bev·ee) n.

. . . .

BILK
(bilk) v.

B

1. gentle, mild, kind; having a beneficial or favorable nature or influence.
2. not harmful or malignant.

Simo's actions toward his competitors was never mean-spirited; he always acted in a benign manner.

. . . .

1. a large group or assemblage.
2. a flock of animals or birds.

There was a bevy of eager bingo fans waiting outside the hall for the game to begin.

. . . .

to deceive or defraud; to swindle, cheat, especially to evade paying one's debts.

The stockbroker was accused of trying to bilk senior citizens out of their investment dollars.

BLASÉ
(blah·'zay) adj.

. . . .

BLASPHEMY
('blas·fě·mee) n.

. . . .

BLATANT
('blay·tant) adj.

1. uninterested because of frequent exposure or indulgence.
2. nonchalant, unconcerned.
3. very sophisticated.

Quincy has traveled so much that he speaks of exotic places such as Borneo in a completely blasé manner.

• •

contemptuous or irreverent acts, utterances, attitudes or writings against God or other things considered sacred; disrespect of something sacrosanct.

If you committed blasphemy during the Inquisition, you were tortured and killed.

• •

completely obvious, not attempting to conceal in any way.

Samuel's blatant disregard of the rules earned him a two-week suspension.

BLIGHT
(blīt) n.

. . . .

BLITHE
(blīth) adj.

. . . .

BOISTEROUS
('boi·stĕ·rŭs) adj.

1. a plant disease that causes the affected parts to wilt and die.
2. something that causes this condition, such as air pollution.
3. something that impairs or destroys.
4. an unsightly object or area.

They still do not know what caused the blight that destroyed half of the trees in the orchard.

. . . .

light-hearted, casual, and carefree.

Rachel's blithe attitude toward spending money left her in debt.

. . . .

1. loud, noisy, and lacking restraint or discipline.
2. stormy and rough.

The boisterous crowd began throwing cups onto the field during the football game.

BOLSTER
('bohl·stĕr) v.

. . . .

BOMBASTIC
(bom·'bas·tik) adj.

. . . .

BOOR
(boor) n.

1. to support or prop up.
2. to buoy or hearten.

Coach Edmond's speech bolstered the team's confidence.

. . . .

speaking pompously, with inflated self-importance.

Ahmed was shocked that a renowned and admired humanitarian could give such a bombastic keynote address.

. . . .

a crude, offensive, ill-mannered person.

Maribel realized she was attending her senior prom with a classic boor when her date wiped his mouth with his sleeve.

BOURGEOIS
(boor·'zhwah) adj.

. . . .

BOWDLERIZE
('bohd·lĕ·rīz) v.

. . . .

BRAVADO
(bră·'vah·doh) n.

typical of the middle class; conforming to the standards and conventions of the middle class; hence also, commonplace, conservative, or materialistic.

Although she won millions in the lottery, Ada still maintains her bourgeois lifestyle.

. . . .

to edit by omitting or modifying parts that may be considered offensive; censor.

The Brothers Grimm had to bowdlerize the folk tales they had collected, for many of the original tales included graphic language, to make their collection of fairy tales suitable for children.

. . . .

false courage, a show of pretended bravery.

Kyle's bravado often got him into trouble with other kids in the neighborhood.

BROACH
(brohch) v.

. . . .

BUMPTIOUS
('bump·shŭs) adj.

. . . .

BUOYANT
('boi·ănt) adj.

B

1. to bring up, introduce, in order to begin a discussion of.
2. to tap or pierce, as in to draw off liquid.

It was hard for Sarah to broach the subject of her mother's weight gain.

. . . .

arrogant, conceited.

The bumptious man could not stop talking about himself or looking in the mirror.

. . . .

1. able to float.
2. light-hearted, cheerful.

In science class, the children tried to identify which objects on the table would be buoyant.

BURGEON
('bur·jŏn) v.

. . . .

BURNISH
('bur·nish) v.

. . . .

to begin to grow and flourish; to begin to sprout, grow new buds, blossom.

The tulip bulbs beneath the soil would burgeon in early spring, providing there was no late frost.

. . . .

to polish, rub to a shine.

When Kathryn began to burnish the old metal tea pot, she realized that it was, in fact, solid silver.

. . . .

CABAL
(kă·'bal) n.

. . . .

CACOPHONY
(kă·'kof·ŏ·nee) n.

. . . .

CADGE
(kaj) v.

1. a scheme or conspiracy.
2. a small group joined in a secret plot.

With Antonio as their leader, the members of the unit secretly readied themselves to begin the cabal.

. . . .

loud, jarring, discordant sound; clamor, din.

I heard a cacophony of instruments coming from the garage where the band was practicing.

. . . .

to beg, to obtain by begging.

Their dog Cleo would cadge at my feet, hoping I would give him table scraps.

CAJOLE
(kă·'johl) v.

. . . .

CANDOR
('kan·dŏr) n.

. . . .

CAPITULATE
(kă·'pich·ŭ·layt) v.

to urge with gentle and repeated appeals or flattery; to wheedle.

Valerie is quite adept at cajoling others to get what she wants, even if it's something she hasn't earned.

· ·

frank, sincere speech; openness.

When I told my boss about my performance concerns, he welcomed my candor.

· ·

to surrender under specific terms or agreed upon conditions; to give in, acquiesce.

Old man Jones was finally ready to capitulate and sell his land to the timber company, but he balked when he saw that he would be compensated for only half of the value of his property.

CAPRICIOUS
(kă·'prish·ŭs) adj.

. . . .

CAREEN
(kă·'reen) v.

. . . .

CASTE
(kast) n.

impulsive, whimsical and unpredictable.

Comedian Robin Williams demonstrates his capricious nature even when he is not performing.

. . . .

1. to lurch from side to side while in motion.
2. to rush carelessly or headlong.

Watching the car in front of us careen down the road was very frightening.

. . . .

a distinct social class or system.

While visiting India, Michael was fascinated to learn the particulars of each caste, and the way they relate to one another.

CASTIGATE
('kas·tĭ·gayt) v.

. . . .

CATHARSIS
(kă·'thahr·sis) n.

. . . .

CAUSTIC
('kaws·tik) adj.

to inflict a severe punishment on; to chastise
severely.

*Bryan's parents castigated him when he was
caught stealing.*

. . . .

the act of ridding or cleansing; relieving
emotions via the experiences of others,
especially through art.

*Survivors of war often experience a catharsis
when viewing Picasso's painting Guernica,
which depicts the bombing of a town during
the Spanish civil war.*

. . . .

1. able to burn, corrode, or dissolve by
chemical action.
2. bitingly sarcastic, cutting.

*The mechanic was very careful when working
with the caustic fluid around the car, because it
could damage the car's paint.*

CENSOR
('sen·sŏr) n.

. . . .

CENSURE
('sen·shŭr) n.

. . . .

an official who reviews books, films, etc. to remove what is considered morally, politically, or otherwise objectionable.

v. to forbid the publication, distribution, or other public dissemination of something because it is considered obscene or otherwise politically or morally unacceptable.

The librarian served as a censor, deciding what books were appropriate for the young readers.

. . . .

expression of strong criticism or disapproval; a rebuke or condemnation.

v. to criticize strongly, rebuke, condemn.

After Tyra was found cheating on the exam, her mother censured her behavior.

. . . .

CHASTISE
('chas·tīz) v.

· ·

CHAUVINIST
('shoh·vĭn·ist) n.

· ·

CHIMERA
(ki·'meer·ă) n.

to punish severely, as with a beating; to criticize harshly, rebuke.

Charles knew his wife would chastise him after he told the roomful of guests she had just had a face lift.

. . . .

a person who believes in the superiority of his or her own kind; an extreme nationalist.

Though common in the early days of the women's movement, male chauvinists are pretty rare today.

. . . .

1. (in Greek mythology) a fire-breathing she-monster with a lion's head; a goat's body; and a serpent's tail.
2. a vain or incongruous fancy; a (monstrous) product of the imagination, illusion.

Seduced by the chimera of immortality, Victor Frankenstein created a monster that ended up destroying him and everyone he loved.

TOEFL iBT® VOCABULARY FLASH REVIEW

CHRONIC
('kron·ik) adj.

. . . .

CHRONICLE
('kron·i·kĕl) n.

. . . .

CHRONOLOGY
(krŏ·'nol·ŏ·jee) n.

C

1. continuing for a long time; on-going, habitual.
2. long-lasting or recurrent.

Seamus had a chronic cough lasting for six months.

. . . .

1. a detailed record or narrative description of past events.

Historians have made a chronicle of the war's events.

. . . .

1. to record in chronological order; make a historical record.

2. the arrangement of events in time; the sequence in which events occur.

The firefighter determined the chronology of incidents that contributed to the fire.

CHRONOMETER
(krŏ·ˈnom·i·těr) n.

. . . .

CHURLISH
(ˈchur·lĭ sh) adj.

. . . .

CIRCUMSPECT
(ˈsur·kŭm·spekt) adj.

C

an exceptionally accurate clock; a precise instrument for measuring time.

The track coach used a chronometer to determine the runner's time for the marathon.

. . . .

ill-mannered, boorish, rude.

Angelo's churlish remarks made everyone at the table uncomfortable.

. . . .

cautious, wary, watchful.

The prison guard was circumspect when he learned that some of the prisoners were planning an escape.

CLANDESTINE
(klan·'des·tin) adj.

. . . .

CLICHÉ
(klee·'shay)

. . . .

COALESCE
(koh·ă·'les) v. n.

conducted in secrecy; kept or done in private, often in order to conceal an illicit or improper purpose.

The private investigator followed Raul to a clandestine rendezvous with a woman in sunglasses and a trench coat.

. . . .

a trite or overused expression or idea.

Tito has an engaging writing style, but he uses too many clichés.

. . . .

to combine and form a whole; to join together, fuse.

The separate islands of Hawaii coalesce to create one state.

COEVAL
(koh·'ee·văl) adj.

. . . .

COGENT
('koh·jĕnt) adj.

. . . .

COLLUSION
(kŏ·'loo·zhŏn) n.

of the same time period, contemporary.

The poet Ben Jonson was coeval to Shakespeare.

. . . .

convincing, persuasive, compelling belief.

Ella's cogent arguments helped the debate team win the state championship.

. . . .

a secret agreement between two or more people for a deceitful or fraudulent purpose; conspiracy.

The discovery of the e-mail proved that the CEO and CFO were in collusion to defraud the shareholders.

COMPLACENT
(kŏm·'play·sĕnt) adj.

. . . .

CONCEDE
(kŏn·'seed) v.

. . . .

CONCILIATORY
(kŏn·'sil·ee·ă·tohr·ee) adj.

C

contented to a fault; self-satisfied,
unconcerned.

*Renee was complacent even when she learned
that her coworkers were trying to get her fired.*

• •

1. to acknowledge or admit as true, proper,
etc. (often with reluctance); to yield, surrender.
2. to grant as a right or privilege.

*The leader conceded the right to vote to all
her country's inhabitants.*

• •

making or willing to make concessions to
reconcile, soothe, or comfort; mollifying,
appeasing.

*Abraham Lincoln made conciliatory gestures
toward the South at the end of the Civil War.*

CONCLAVE
('kon·klav) n.

. . . .

CONSENSUS
(kŏn·'sen·sŭs) n.

. . . .

CONSTERNATION
(kon·stĕr·'nay·shŏn) n.

a private or secret meeting.

The double agent had a conclave with the spy he was supposed to be observing.

• •

general agreement or accord; an opinion or position reached by a group.

The school board reached a consensus about building a new high school.

• •

a feeling of deep, incapacitating horror or dismay.

The look of consternation on the faces of the students taking the history exam alarmed the teacher, who thought he had prepared them for the test.

CONTENTIOUS
(kŏn·'ten·shŭs) adj.

. . . .

CONUNDRUM
(kŏ·'nun·drŭm) n.

. . . .

COPIOUS
('koh·pi·ŭs) adj.

1. quarrelsome, competitive, quick to fight.
2. controversial, causing contention.

With two contentious candidates on hand, it was sure to be a lively debate.

. . . .

a hard riddle, enigma; a puzzling question or problem.

Alex's logic professor gave the class a conundrum to work on over the weekend.

. . . .

large in number or quantity; abundant, plentiful.

The shipwrecked couple found a copious supply of coconut trees and shellfish on the island.

CORNUCOPIA
(kor·nyŭ·ˈkoh·pi·ă) n.

. . . .

CORROBORATE
(kŏ·ˈrob·ŏ·rayt) v.

. . . .

COUNTENANCE
(ˈkown·tĕ·năns) n.

C

abundance; a horn of plenty.

The first graders made cornucopias for Thanksgiving by placing papier-mâché vegetables into a hollowed-out horn.

. . . .

to strengthen or support with evidence or authority; to make more certain, confirm.

Both Irma's and Ye's statements corroborate Tia's story, so she must be telling the truth.

. . . .

the appearance of a person's face, facial features and expression.

All of the wedding guests could see the bride's radiant countenance as she walked down the aisle.

CRAVEN
('kray·věn) adj.

· ·

CREDULOUS
('krej·ŭ·lŭs) adj.

· ·

CRUX
(kruks) n.

cowardly.

"This craven act of violence will not go unpunished," remarked the police chief.

. . . .

gullible; too willing to believe things.

All the tables, graphs, and charts made the company's assets very appealing to the credulous potential investors at the meeting.

. . . .

the central or critical point or feature, especially of a problem.

The crux of the trial was her whereabouts at the time of the burglary.

CRYPTIC
('krip·tik) adj.

. . . .

CUE
(kyoo) n.

. . . .

having a hidden or secret meaning, mysterious; hidden, secret, occult.

Jimmy was confused by the cryptic note he found written on the refrigerator.

. . . .

1. a signal, such as a word or action, given to prompt or remind someone of something; a hint or suggestion.
2. a line of waiting people or vehicles; a queue.

When the timer buzzed, Sonia realized that was her cue to take the hamburgers off the grill.

. . . .

CULPABLE
('kul·pă·běl) adj.

. . . .

CURSORY
('kur·sŏ·ree) adj.

. . . .

deserving blame or censure for being or doing something wrong or harmful; blameworthy, guilty.

I admitted I was culpable when my prank ended up breaking Andrea's lamp.

. . . .

hasty and superficial.

Although I should have proofread the essay carefully, I only had time to give it a cursory review.

. . . .

DAUNT
(dawnt) v.

. . . .

DEBACLE
(di·'bah·kěl) n.

. . . .

DEBUT
(day·'byoo) n.

D

to intimidate, to make afraid or discouraged.

His austere manner daunted the small children.

· ·

1. a sudden disaster or collapse; a total defeat or failure.
2. a sudden breaking up or breaking loose; violent flood waters, often caused by the breaking up of ice in a river.

Putting the bridge's supporting beams in loose sand caused a total debacle when the sand shifted and the bridge fell apart.

· ·

a first appearance in or presentation to the public.
v. to make a first appearance in public.

Irina's Carnegie Hall debut received rave reviews.

DECIMATE
('des·ĭ·mayt) v.

. . . .

DECORUM
(di·'kohr·ŭm) n.

. . . .

DE FACTO
(dee 'fak·toh) adj. & adv.

to destroy a large portion of.

Neglect and time will eventually decimate much of the housing in inner cities.

• •

appropriateness of behavior, propriety; decency in manners and conduct.

Concerning questions of decorum, I always refer to Emily Post.

• •

in reality or fact; actual.

The king is only the nominal head of the country; the de facto leader is the prime minister.

DEIGN
(dayn) v.

. . . .

DELINEATE
(di·'lin·ee·ayt) v.

. . . .

DELUDE
(di·'lood) v.

D

to condescend, to be kind or gracious enough to do something thought to be beneath one's dignity.

Would you deign to spare a dime for a poor old beggar like me?

· ·

to draw or outline, sketch; to clearly portray, depict, describe.

The survey will delineate where their property ends.

· ·

to deceive, make someone believe something that is wrong.

Nicole deluded Maria when she claimed to forgive her.

DEMAGOGUE

('dem·ă·gawg) n.

. . . .

DEMUR

(di·'mur) v.

. . . .

DEMURE

(di·'myoor) adj.

D

a political leader who obtains power by appealing to people's feelings and prejudices rather than by reasoning.

The dictator was widely regarded as an infamous demagogue.

· ·

to raise objections, hesitate.

Polly hated to demur, but she didn't think adding ten cloves of garlic to the recipe would taste good.

· ·

modest and shy, or pretending to be so.

When it was to her advantage, Sharon could be very demure, but otherwise she was quite outgoing.

DENIGRATE
('den·i·grayt) v.

. . . .

DENOUEMENT
(day·noo·'mahn) n.

. . . .

DEPRECATE
('dep·rĕ·kayt) v.

D

to blacken the reputation of, disparage, defame.

The movie script reportedly contained scenes that would denigrate the queen, so those scenes were removed.

• •

the resolution or clearing up of the plot at the end of a narrative; the outcome or solution of an often complex series of events.

The story's denouement answered many of the student's questions.

• •

to express disapproval of; to belittle, depreciate.

Grandpa's tendency to deprecate the children's friends was a frequent source of family strife.

DERISIVE
(di·ˈrī·siv) adj.

. . . .

DERIVATIVE
(di·ˈriv·ă·tiv) n.

. . . .

DESECRATE
(ˈdes·ĕ·krayt) v.

scornful, expressing ridicule; mocking, jeering.

Derisive comments were forbidden in the classroom, and students were encouraged to speak freely.

something that is derived or made by derivation.

adj. derived from another source, unoriginal.

The word "atomic" is a derivative of the word "atom."

to violate the sacredness of, to profane.

Someone desecrated the local cemetery by spray-painting graffiti on tombstones.

DESTITUTE
('des·ti·toot) adj.

. . . .

DESULTORY
('des·ŭl·tohr·ee) adj.

. . . .

DETRACT
(di·'trakt) v.

D

1. penniless, extremely poor.
2. utterly lacking.

After the economy declined, many families were left destitute.

. . . .

aimless, haphazard; moving from one subject to another without logical connection.

Ichabod's desultory ramblings made coherent conversation difficult.

. . . .

to draw or take away from; to remove part of something, diminish.

Unfortunately, Helen's slovenly appearance detracted from the impact of her otherwise brilliant presentation.

DICHOTOMY
(dī·ˈkot·ŏ·mee) n.

. . . .

DIFFIDENT
(ˈdif·i·dĕnt) adj.

. . . .

DIFFUSE
(di·ˈfyooz) v.

TOEFL iBT® VOCABULARY FLASH REVIEW

D

division into two contradictory parts or groups.

When the teacher broached the subject of politics with her students, there was a predictable dichotomy between liberal and conservative.

. . . .

lacking self-confidence, shy and timid.

Alan used to be so diffident, but now he's the life of the party.

. . . .

1. to spread throughout, disperse, extend.
2. to soften, make less brilliant.
adj. 1. spread out, scattered, not concentrated.
2. wordy, verbose.

The perfume she sprayed diffused throughout her bedroom.

DIGRESS
(dī·'gres) v.

. . . .

DILATORY
('dil·ă·tohr·ee) adj.

. . . .

DISABUSE
(dis·ă·'byooz) v.

D

to turn aside, deviate, or swerve; to stray from the main subject in writing or speaking.

Her argument digressed from the main problem she had about her friend's spending habits.

• •

slow or late in doing something; intended to delay, especially to gain time.

Miguel's dilatory approach to getting himself up and dressed was his own small act of passive resistance to having to work on a holiday.

• •

to undeceive, correct a false impression or erroneous belief.

Natalie needed to disabuse Chin of his belief that she was in love with him.

DISCERN
(di·'surn) v.

. . . .

DISCONCERT
(dis·kŏn·'surt) v.

. . . .

DISCONSOLATE
(dis·'kon·sŏ·lit) adj.

to perceive clearly; to distinguish, recognize as being distinct.

Remy discerned that Opal had no intention of calling him back.

. . . .

1. to upset the composure of, to ruffle.
2. to frustrate plans by throwing into disorder.

The arrival of Miriam's ex-husband and his new wife managed to disconcert the typically unflappable Miriam.

. . . .

1. sad, dejected, disappointed.
2. inconsolable, hopelessly unhappy.

The disconsolate look on Peter's face revealed the letter contained bad news.

DISDAIN
(dis·'dayn) n.

. . . .

DISENFRANCHISE
(dis·en·'fran·chīz) v.

. . . .

DISINGENUOUS
(dis·in·'jen·yoo·ŭs) adj.

a feeling or showing of haughty contempt or scorn; a state of being despised.

v. 1. to regard with haughty contempt or scorn, to despise.

   2. to consider or reject (someone or something) as unworthy or beneath one's dignity.

I was humiliated by the way Angelica disdained every idea I proposed at that meeting.

· ·

to deprive of the rights of citizenship, especially the right to vote.

The independent monitors were at polling locations to ensure neither party tried to disenfranchise incoming voters.

· ·

1. insincere, calculating; not straightforward or frank.

2. falsely pretending to be unaware.

Carl's disingenuous comments were not taken seriously by anyone in the room.

DISPARAGE
(di·ˈspar·ij) v.

. . . .

DISSIPATE
(ˈdis·ĭ·payt) v.

. . . .

DISSEMBLE
(di·ˈsem·běl) v.

to speak of in a slighting or derogatory way, to belittle.

Comedians often disparage politicians as part of their comedic routines.

. . . .

1. to separate and scatter completely; to disperse to the point of disappearing, or nearly so.
2. to be extravagant and wasteful, especially in the pursuit of pleasure; squander.

The crowd dissipated when the riot police arrived.

. . . .

to disguise or conceal one's true feelings or motives behind a false appearance.

Tom needed to dissemble his goal of taking his boss's job by acting supportive of his boss's planned job change.

DISSUADE
(di·'swayd) v.

. . . .

DITHER
('dith·ĕr) v.

. . . .

DOGMA
('dawg·mă) n.

D

to discourage from or persuade against a course of action.

I tried to dissuade them from painting their house purple, but they didn't listen.

. . . .

1. to hesitate, be indecisive and uncertain.
2. to shake or quiver.

It is important to have a leader who will not dither during a crisis.

. . . .

a system of principles or beliefs, a prescribed doctrine.

Some find the inherent dogma in religion a comfort, whereas others find it too restrictive.

DORMANT
('dor·mănt) adj.

. . . .

DRACONIAN
(dray·'koh·ni·ăn) adj.

. . . .

DROLL
(drohl) adj.

D

1. lying asleep or as if asleep, inactive, at rest.
2. inactive but capable of becoming active; latent, temporarily quiescent.

The geology students made a surprising discovery: The volcano believed to be dormant was about to erupt.

. . . .

very harsh, extremely severe (especially a law or punishment).

Students of international policy are often shocked by the draconian punishments used by other countries for seemingly minor offenses.

. . . .

amusing in an odd or whimsical way.

This is a wonderful, droll story—the children will love it!

DROSS
(draws) n.

. . . .

DULCET
('dul·sit) adj.

. . . .

DUPE
(doop) n.

1. waste product, sludge.
2. something worthless, commonplace, or trivial.

Work crews immediately began the task of clearing the dross at the abandoned plastics factory.

. . . .

melodious, harmonious, sweet-sounding.

The chamber orchestra's dulcet tunes were a perfect end to a great evening.

. . . .

someone who is easily deceived, gullible.
v. to deceive, trick.

Charlene was duped into buying this lemon of a car by a slick-talking salesman.

E

EBB
(eb) n.

. . . .

EBULLIENT
(i·ˈbul·yĕnt) adj.

. . . .

ECCENTRIC
(ik·ˈsen·trik) adj.

TOEFL iBT® VOCABULARY FLASH REVIEW

the return of the tide to the sea.

v. 1. to flow back or recede, as the tide.
2. to fall back, decline.

I hope Mark's anger has ebbed; I am eager for a reconciliation.

. . . .

bubbling over with enthusiasm, exuberant.

The ebullient children were eager to stick their hands into the grab bag and pull out a toy.

. . . .

deviating from the conventional or established norm or pattern; anomalous, irregular.

Her artwork was unlike any other artist at the museum; each painting had its own eccentric color scheme.

ECLECTIC
(i·'klek·tik) adj.

. . . .

ÉCLAT
(ay·'klah) n.

. . . .

EDIFYING
('ed·ĭ·fi·ing) adj.

E

1. selecting or employing elements from a variety of sources, systems, or styles.
2. consisting of elements from a variety of sources.

You're sure to meet someone interesting at the party—Marieka always invites an eclectic group of people to her gatherings.

. . . .

conspicuous success; great acclaim or applause; brilliant performance or achievement.

Even the ruinous deceit of the envious Salieri could not impede the dazzling éclat of the young and gifted Mozart.

. . . .

enlightening or uplifting with the aim of improving intellectual or moral development; instructing, improving.

His edifying speech challenged the audience to devote more time to charitable causes.

EFFICACIOUS
(ef·ĭ·ˈkay·shŭs) adj.

· ·

EFFRONTERY
(i·ˈfrun·tĕ·ree) n.

· ·

EFFUSIVE
(i·ˈfyoo·siv) adj.

acting effectively, producing the desired effect or result.

Margaret's efficacious approach to her job made her a favorite with the CFO.

· ·

brazen boldness, impudence, insolence.

The customs officials were infuriated by the effrontery of the illegal alien who nonchalantly carried drugs into the country in his shirt pocket.

· ·

expressing emotions in an unrestrained or excessive way; profuse, overflowing, gushy.

Anne's unexpectedly effusive greeting made Tammy uncomfortable.

EGALITARIAN
(i·gal·i·ˈtair·ee·ăn) adj.

. . . .

EGREGIOUS
(i·ˈgree·jŭs) adj.

. . . .

EKE
(eek) v.

characterized by or affirming the principle of equal political, social, civil, and economic rights for all persons.

Hannah was moved by the candidate's egalitarian speech.

. . . .

conspicuously and outrageously bad or offensive; flagrant.

Enis was fired after her egregious accounting error cost the company thousands of dollars.

. . . .

to get or supplement with great effort or strain; to earn or accomplish laboriously.

Working two jobs enabled Quincy to eke out a living wage for his family.

ÉLAN
(ay·'lahn) n.

....

ELITE
(i·'leet) n.

....

ELOQUENT
('el·ŏ·kwĕnt) adj.

E

1. vivacity, enthusiasm, vigor.
2. distinctive style or flair.

The designer's élan and originality helped him succeed in the highly competitive fashion industry.

. . . .

1. the best or most skilled members of a social group or class.
2. a person or group regarded as superior.

Within the student orchestra, there existed a small group of musical elite who performed around the country.

. . . .

expressing strong emotions or arguments in a powerful, fluent, and persuasive manner.

Abraham Lincoln's Gettysburg Address is considered one of the most eloquent speeches ever given by a U.S. president.

ELUSIVE
(i·'loo·siv) adj.

· ·

EMINENT
('em·ĭ·nĕnt) adj.

· ·

EMPIRICAL
(em·'pir·i·kal) adj.

evasive, eluding the grasp; difficult to capture, describe or comprehend.

The elusive bank robber was not caught during his crime spree.

. . . .

towering above or more prominent than others, lofty; standing above others in quality, character, reputation, etc.; distinguished.

The chairperson proudly announced that the keynote speaker at the animal rights convention would be the eminent primatologist Jane Goodall.

. . . .

based on observation or experience rather than theory.

Frank's empirical data suggested that mice would climb over the walls of the maze to get to the cheese, rather than navigate the maze itself.

EMULATE
('em·yŭ·layt) v.

. . . .

ENCLAVE
('en·klayv) n.

. . . .

ENDEMIC
(en·'dem·ik) adj.

E

to try to equal or excel, especially by imitation.

Ricky admired his sister Joan and always tried to emulate her behavior.

• •

a distinct territory lying wholly within the boundaries of another, larger territory.

The country of Lesotho is an enclave of South Africa.

• •

1. prevalent in or characteristic of a specific area or group of people.
2. native to a particular region.

Kudzu, a hairy, purple-flowered vine thought to be endemic to the southeastern United States, was actually imported from Japan.

E

ENERVATE
('en·ĕr·vayt) v.

. . . .

ENGENDER
(en·'jen·dĕr) v.

. . . .

ENIGMA
(ĕ·'nig·mă) n.

TOEFL iBT® VOCABULARY FLASH REVIEW

E

to weaken or deprive of strength or vitality; to make feeble or impotent.

Stephanie's cutting remarks managed to enervate Hasaan.

. . . .

to produce, give rise to, bring into existence.

Professor Sorenson's support worked to engender Samantha's desire to pursue a PhD.

. . . .

something that is puzzling or difficult to understand; a baffling problem or riddle.

The math problem was difficult to solve and proved to be an enigma.

TOEFL iBT® VOCABULARY FLASH REVIEW

ENNUI
(ahn·'wee) n.

· ·

ENORMITY
(i·'nor·mi·tee) n.

· ·

ENSCONCE
(en·'skons) v.

boredom and listlessness resulting from something tedious or uninteresting.

The tour guide's façade of enthusiasm could not hide his ennui.

. . . .

1. a monstrous offense or evil act, atrocity.
2. excessive wickedness.
(Note: Enormity is often used to indicate something of great size—e.g., the enormity of the task—but this is considered an incorrect use of the word.)

The enormity of the serial killer's crimes will never be forgotten.

. . . .

1. to fix or settle firmly and securely.
2. to place or hide securely, conceal.

Once the spy was comfortably ensconced in his new identity, he began his secret mission.

EPHEMERAL
(i·ˈfem·ĕ·răl) adj.

· ·

EPICUREAN
(ep·i·ˈkyoor·ee·ăn) n.

· ·

EPIPHANY
(i·ˈpif·ă·nee) n.

lasting only a very short time, transitory.

Summer always seems so ephemeral; before you know it, it's time to go back to school.

. . . .

a person devoted to the pursuit of pleasure and luxury, especially the enjoyment of good food and comfort.

While on vacation at a posh resort hotel, Joan became a true epicurean.

. . . .

1. a sudden, intuitive realization of the essence or meaning of something, a perceptive revelation.
2. a manifestation of the divine.
3. Epiphany, a Christian feast on the twelfth day after Christmas celebrating the divine manifestation of Jesus to the Magi.

As I listened to Professor Lane's lecture, I had an epiphany that I was in the wrong major.

EPITOME
(i·ˈpit·ŏ·mee) n.

. . . .

EQUANIMITY
(ee·kwă·ˈnim·i·tee) n.

. . . .

EQUIVOCATE
(i·ˈkwiv·ŏ·kayt) v.

E

1. something or someone that embodies a particular quality or characteristic, a representative example or a typical model.
2. a brief summary or abstract.

Einstein is the epitome of true genius.

. . . .

calmness of temperament, even-temperedness; patience and composure, especially under stressful circumstances.

The hostage negotiator's equanimity during the standoff was remarkable.

. . . .

to use unclear or ambiguous language in order to mislead or conceal the truth.

Raj equivocated when explaining why he came home after his curfew.

ERADICATE
(i·'rad·ĭ·kayt) v.

. . . .

ERRATIC
(i·'rat·ik) adj.

. . . .

ERSATZ
(ĕr·'zăts) adj.

E

to root out and utterly destroy; to annihilate, exterminate.

The exterminator said he would eradicate the vermin from the house.

. . . .

1. moving or behaving in an irregular, uneven, or inconsistent manner.
2. deviating from the normal or typical course of action, opinion, etc.

During an earthquake, a seismograph's needle moves in an erratic manner.

. . . .

artificial; being an imitation or substitute, especially one that is inferior.

Though most of the guests couldn't tell the difference, Waldo knew that the dish was made with ersatz truffles.

ERUDITE
('er·yŭ·dīt) adj.

. . . .

ETHOS
('ee·thos) n.

. . . .

EULOGY
('yoo·lŏ·gee) n.

having or showing great learning; profoundly educated, scholarly.

The scholarly work of nonfiction was obviously written by an erudite young man.

· ·

the spirit, attitude, disposition, or beliefs characteristic of a community, epoch, region, etc.

The ethos of their group included a commitment to pacifism.

· ·

a formal speech or piece of writing in praise of someone who has died.

Richard was asked to give a eulogy for his fallen comrade.

EUPHORIA
(yoo·ˈfohr·ee·aˇ) n.

· ·

EVADE
(i·ˈvayd) v.

· ·

EVANESCENT
(ev·ăˇ·ˈnes·ĕnt) adj.

E

a feeling of well-being or high spirits.

When falling in love, it is not uncommon to experience feelings of euphoria.

· ·

1. to elude or avoid by cleverness or deceit.
2. to avoid fulfilling, answering, or doing.

The thief evaded the store's security guards by escaping out the back door.

· ·

vanishing or tending to vanish like vapor; transitory, fleeting.

The subject of the poem is the evanescent nature of young love.

EVINCE
(i·'vins) v.

. . . .

EXACERBATE
(ig·'zas·ĕr·bayt) v.

. . . .

EXCULPATE
(eks·'kul·payt) v.

to show or demonstrate clearly; to make evident.

The safety officer tried to evince the dangers of driving under the influence by showing pictures of alcohol-related automobile accidents.

. . . .

to make worse; to increase the severity, violence, or bitterness of.

We should have known that splashing salt water on Dan's wound would exacerbate his pain.

. . . .

to free from blame, to clear from a charge of guilt.

When Anthony admitted to the crime, it served to exculpate Marcus.

EXIGENT
('ek·si·jĕnt) adj.

. . . .

EXORBITANT
(ig·'zor·bi·tănt) adj.

. . . .

EXPEDIENT
(ik·'spee·dee·ĕnt) n.

1. urgent, requiring immediate action or attention, critical.
2. requiring much effort or precision, demanding.

The late-night call on Paul's cell phone concerned matters of an exigent nature.

. . . .

greatly exceeding the bounds of what is normal or reasonable; inordinate and excessive.

Three thousand dollars is an exorbitant amount to pay for a scarf.

. . . .

a short-lived means to an end.

adj. 1. appropriate for a purpose, suitable for a means to an end.
2. serving to promote one's own interests rather than principle.

A quick divorce was an expedient end to the couple's two-month marriage.

EXPLICIT
(ik·'splis·it) adj.

. . . .

EXPUNGE
(ik·'spunj) v.

. . . .

EXTENUATE
(ik·ten·'yoo·ayt) v.

E

stated clearly and fully; straightforward, exact.

*The terms of the rental agreement were
explicit in the document.*

. . . .

to wipe or rub out, delete; to eliminate
completely, annihilate.

*After finishing probation, juveniles can petition
the courts to expunge their criminal records.*

. . . .

to reduce the strength or lessen the
seriousness of, to try to partially excuse.

The man's desperation extenuated his actions.

FAÇADE
(fă·'sahd) n.

. . . .

FACETIOUS
(fă·'see·shŭs) adj.

. . . .

FALLACY
('fal·ă·see) n.

F

1. the face or front of a building.
2. an artificial or deceptive front, especially one intended to hide something unpleasant.

Antoine's stoicism is just a façade; he is a deeply emotional person.

· ·

humorous and witty, cleverly amusing; jocular, sportive.

Jude's facetious reply angered his teacher but made his classmates laugh.

· ·

1. a false notion or misconception resulting from incorrect or illogical reasoning.
2. that which is deceptive or has a false appearance; something that misleads, deception.

The "slippery slope" fallacy argues that once X happens, Y and Z will automatically follow.

FATUOUS
('fach·oo·ŭs) adj.

....

FECKLESS
('fek·lis) adj.

....

FECUND
('fek·ŭnd) adj.

complacently stupid; feeble-minded and silly.

Because Sam was such an intellectually accomplished student, Mr. Britt was surprised to discover that Sam's well-meaning but fatuous parents were not at all like him.

· ·

1. lacking purpose or vitality; feeble, weak.
2. incompetent and ineffective, careless.

Jake's feckless performance led to his termination from the team.

· ·

fertile.

The fecund soil in the valley was able to sustain the growing garden.

FEIGN
(fayn) v.

. . . .

FELICITOUS
(fi·'lis·i·tŭs) adj.

. . . .

FERVOR
('fur·vŏr) n.

to pretend, to give the false appearance of.

Walter feigned illness to avoid attending the meeting.

. . . .

1. apt, suitably expressed, apropos.
2. marked by good fortune.

The felicitous turn of events during her promotional tour propelled Susan's book to the best-seller list.

. . . .

zeal, ardor, intense emotion.

The fervor of the fans in the stands helped propel the team to victory.

FETTER
('fet·ĕr) v.

. . . .

FLACCID
('fla·sid) adj.

. . . .

FLIPPANT
('flip·ănt) adj.

F

1. to impede or restrict.
2. to shackle, put in chains.

The presence of two security guards fettered their plans to get backstage.

. . . .

hanging loose or wrinkled; weak, flabby, not firm.

The skin of cadavers becomes flaccid in a matter of hours.

. . . .

not showing proper seriousness; disrespectful, saucy.

Ursula's flippant remarks in front of her fiancé's parents were an embarrassment to all.

FLORID
('flor·id) adj.

....

FLOUT
(flowt) v.

....

FORBEARANCE
(for·'bair·ăns) n.

1. elaborate, ornate.
2. (of complexion) ruddy, rosy.

The florid architecture in Venice did not appeal to me; I prefer buildings without so much ornamentation.

. . . .

to disobey openly and scornfully; to reject, mock, go against (as in a tradition or convention).

Flappers in the early twentieth century flouted convention by bobbing their hair and wearing very short skirts.

. . . .

patience, willingness to wait, tolerance.

Gustaf dreaded the security check in the airport, but he faced it with great forbearance because he knew it was for his own safety.

FORESTALL
(fohr·'stawl) v.

. . . .

FORSWEAR
(for·'swair) v.

. . . .

FORTUITOUS
(for·'too·i·tŭs) adj.

F

to prevent by taking action first, preempt.

The diplomat was able to forestall a conflict by holding secret meetings with both parties.

• •

1. to give up, renounce.
2. to deny under oath.

Natasha had to forswear her allegiance to her homeland in order to become a citizen of the new country.

• •

happening by accident or chance; occurring unexpectedly or without any known cause. (Note: *Fortuitous* is commonly used to mean a happy accident or an unexpected but fortunate occurrence. In its true sense, however, a fortuitous event can be either fortunate or unfortunate.)

By a stroke of fortuitous bad luck, Wei chose a small, exclusive resort for her vacation—only to find that the ex-boyfriend she wanted to get away from had also chosen the same resort.

FRUGAL
('froo·găl) adj.

....

FULMINATE
('ful·mĭ·nayt) v.

....

FULSOME
('fuul·sŏm) adj.

F

1. careful and economical, sparing, thrifty.
2. costing little.

My grandparents survived the Great Depression by being very frugal.

....

1. to issue a thunderous verbal attack, berate.
2. to explode or detonate.

The senator liked to fulminate when other legislators questioned her ideology.

....

offensive due to excessiveness, especially excess flattery or praise.

Her new coworker's fulsome attention bothered Kathryn.

FURTIVE
('fur·tiv) adj.

. . . .

FUTILE
('fyoo·tīl) adj.

. . . .

F

1. characterized by stealth or secrecy, surreptitious.
2. suggesting a hidden motive, shifty.

Harriet's furtive glance told me I had better keep quiet about what I had just seen.

· ·

useless, producing no result; hopeless, vain.

Arguing with my mother was futile, as she would never let me attend the party.

· ·

GAINSAY
('gayn·say) v.

. . . .

GARGANTUAN
(gahr·'gan·choo·ăn) adj.

. . . .

GARISH
('gair·ish) adj.

Petra would gainsay all accusations made against her.

. . . .

gigantic, huge.

It was a gargantuan supermarket for such a small town.

. . . .

excessively bright or over-decorated, gaudy; tastelessly showy.

Though Susan thought Las Vegas was garish, Emily thought it was perfectly beautiful.

GARNER
('gahr·něr) v.

. . . .

GARRULOUS
('gar·ŭ·lŭs) adj.

. . . .

GAUCHE
(gohsh) adj.

G

to gather and store up; to amass, acquire.

Whitney garnered enough money to buy a used car.

. . . .

talkative.

Aunt Midge is as garrulous as they come, so be prepared to listen for hours.

. . . .

1. lacking social graces or polish; without tact.
2. clumsy or awkward.

My little brother is so gauche that it's embarrassing to be with him in public.

TOEFL iBT® VOCABULARY FLASH REVIEW

GENTEEL
(jen·'teel) adj.

. . . .

GERRYMANDER
('jer·i·man·děr) n.

. . . .

GESTALT
(gě·shtălt) n.

TOEFL iBT® VOCABULARY FLASH REVIEW

elegantly polite, well bred, refined.

The genteel host made sure that each entrée was cooked to each guest's specifications.

. . . .

the act of gerrymandering.

v. to divide an area into voting districts so as to give one party an unfair advantage.

The election was rigged by gerrymandering, thus ensuring the incumbent's reelection.

. . . .

a configuration or pattern of elements so unified as a whole that it cannot be described merely as a sum of its parts.

One of the fundamental beliefs of gestalt therapy is that we exist in a web of relationships to other things, and that it is possible to understand ourselves only in the context of these relationships.

GIRD
(gurd) v.

. . . .

GREGARIOUS
(grĕ·'gair·ee·ŭs) adj.

. . . .

GROVEL
('gruv·ĕl) v.

G

1. to encircle or bind with a belt or band.
2. to encompass, surround.
3. to prepare for action, especially military confrontation.
4. to sneer at, mock, gibe.

The negotiations had failed, so the soldiers girded for battle.

. . . .

1. seeking and enjoying the company of others, sociable.
2. tending to form a group with others of the same kind.

Alan used to be so diffident, but now he's as gregarious as can be and is usually the life of the party.

. . . .

to lie or creep with one's face to the ground in a servile, humble, or fearful manner.

Panji, if you want your boss to treat you with respect, you've got to stop groveling and stand up for yourself.

GUFFAW
(gu·ˈfaw) n.

. . . .

GUILE
(gīl) n.

. . . .

G

a noisy, coarse burst of laughter.

Michael let out quite a guffaw when Jamal told him the outlandish joke.

. . . .

treacherous cunning; shrewd, crafty deceit.

The most infamous pirates displayed tremendous guile.

. . . .

HALLOW
('hal·oh) v.

. . . .

HAPLESS
('hap·lis) adj.

. . . .

HARANGUE
(hă·'rang) n.

H

to make holy, consecrate.

The religious leader hallowed the new worship hall.

⋯⋯⋯⋯⋯⋯⋯⋯⋯⋯⋯⋯⋯⋯⋯⋯⋯

unlucky, unfortunate.

The hapless circumstances of her journey resulted in lost luggage, missed connections, and a very late arrival.

⋯⋯⋯⋯⋯⋯⋯⋯⋯⋯⋯⋯⋯⋯⋯⋯⋯

a long, often scolding or bombastic speech; a tirade.

v. to speak in a pompous maner; to declaim.

Members of the audience began to get restless during the senator's political harangue.

HARBINGER
('hahr·bin·jĕr) n.

· ·

HARROWING
('har·oh·ing) adj.

· ·

HAUGHTY
('haw·tee) adj.

a person, thing, or event that foreshadows or indicates what is to come; a forerunner or precursor.

The arrival of the robins is a harbinger of spring.

. . . .

distressing, creating great stress or torment.

The turbulent flight proved to be a harrowing experience for Jane.

. . . .

scornfully arrogant and condescending; acting as though one is superior and others unworthy, disdainful.

Stanley's haughty attitude means that he has very few friends.

HEGEMONY
(hi·'jem·ŏ·nee) n.

. . . .

HERMETIC
(hur·'met·ik) adj.

. . . .

HIATUS
(hī·'ay·tŭs) n.

predominant influence or leadership, especially of one government over others.

The hegemony of his country borders on imperialism.

. . . .

1. having an airtight closure.
2. protected from outside influences.

In the hermetic world of the remote mountain village, the inhabitants did not even know that their country was on the brink of war.

. . . .

a gap or opening; an interruption or break.

After he was laid off by the bank, Kobitu decided to take a long hiatus from the financial world and took a job as a middle school math teacher.

HONE
(hohn) v.

. . . .

HUBRIS

('hyoo·bris) n.

. . . .

to sharpen; to perfect, make more effective.

By practicing creating spreadsheets, I honed my computer skills.

. . . .

overbearing pride or presumption.

In the Greek tragedy Oedipus Rex, *Oedipus's hubris leads to his downfall.*

. . . .

ICONOCLAST
(ī·'kon·oh·klast) n.

. . . .

IGNOBLE
(ig·'noh·běl) adj.

. . . .

IGNOMINIOUS
(ig·nŏ·'min·ee·ŭs) adj.

1. a person who attacks and seeks to overthrow traditional ideas, beliefs, or institutions.
2. someone who opposes and destroys idols used in worship.

Using words as weapons, the well-spoken iconoclast challenged political hypocrisy and fanaticism wherever she found it.

. . . .

1. lacking nobility in character or purpose, dishonorable.
2. not of the nobility, common.

Mark was an ignoble successor to such a well-respected leader, so many members of the organization resigned in protest.

. . . .

1. marked by shame or disgrace.
2. deserving disgrace or shame; despicable.

The evidence of plagiarism brought an ignominious end to what had been a notable career for the talented young author.

IMBROGLIO
(im·'brohl·yoh) n.

. . . .

IMMOLATE
('im·ŏ·layt) v.

. . . .

IMPASSE
('im·pas) n.

I

a confused or difficult situation, usually involving a disagreement or misunderstanding.

In Shakespeare's comedies, there is often an imbroglio caused by a case of mistaken identity.

. . . .

1. to kill, as a sacrifice.
2. to kill (oneself) by fire.
3. to destroy (one thing for another).

In order for the plants to grow, I had to immolate the weeds.

. . . .

a deadlock, stalemate; a difficulty without a solution.

The labor negotiations with management reached an impasse, and a strike seemed imminent.

IMPASSIVE
(im·'pas·iv) adj.

. . . .

IMPECUNIOUS
(im·pě·'kyoo·nee·ŭs) adj.

. . . .

IMPERIALISM
(im·'peer·ee·ă·liz·ěm) n.

I

not showing or feeling emotion or pain.

It was hard to know what she was feeling by looking at the impassive expression on her face.

· ·

having little or no money; poor, penniless.

Many impecunious immigrants to the United States are eventually able to make comfortable lives for themselves.

· ·

the policy of extending the rule or authority of a nation or empire by acquiring other territories or dependencies.

Great Britain embraced imperialism, acquiring so many territories that the sun never set on the British Empire.

IMPERIOUS
(im·ˈpeer·ee·ŭs) adj.

. . . .

IMPERVIOUS
(im·ˈpur·vee·ŭs) adj.

. . . .

IMPETUOUS
(im·ˈpech·oo·u̬s) adj.

overbearing, bossy, domineering.

Stella was relieved with her new job transfer because she would no longer be under the control of such an imperious boss.

. . . .

1. incapable of being penetrated.
2. not able to be influenced or affected.

Hadley is such a die-hard libertarian that he is impervious to any attempts to change his beliefs.

. . . .

1. characterized by sudden, forceful energy or emotion; impulsive, unduly hasty and without thought.
2. marked by violent force.

It was an impetuous decision to run off to Las Vegas and get married after a one-week courtship.

IMPLACABLE
(im·ˈplak·ă·běl) adj.

. . . .

IMPORTUNE
(im·por·ˈtoon) v.

. . . .

IMPRECATION
(im·prě·ˈkay·shŏn) n.

incapable of being placated or appeased;
inexorable.

*Some of the people who call the customer
service desk for assistance are implacable, but
most are relatively easy to serve.*

. . . .

1. to ask incessantly, make incessant requests.
2. to beg persistently and urgently.

*Children can't help but importune during the
holidays, constantly nagging for the toys they
see advertised on television.*

. . . .

an invocation of evil, a curse.

*In the book I'm reading, the gypsy queen
levies an imprecation on the lead character.*

IMPUDENT
('im·pyŭ·dĕnt) adj.

. . . .

IMPUGN
(im·'pyoon) v.

. . . .

IMPUTE
(im·'pyoot) v.

1. boldly showing a lack of respect, insolent.
2. shamelessly forward, immodest.

Thumbing his nose at the principal was an impudent act.

. . . .

to attack as false or questionable; to contradict or call into question.

The editorial impugned the senator's reelection platform, and set the tone for the upcoming debate.

. . . .

to attribute to a cause or source, ascribe, credit.

Doctors impute the reduction in cancer deaths to the nationwide decrease in cigarette smoking.

INCENSE
('in·sens) n.

. . . .

INCENDIARY
(in·'sen·dee·er·ee) adj.

. . . .

INCHOATE
(in·'koh·it) adj.

fragrant material that gives off scents when burned. (in·'sens)

v. to make (someone) angry.

Marcel's criticism incensed his coworker.

· ·

1. causing or capable of causing fire; burning readily.
2. of or involving arson.
3. tending to incite or inflame, inflammatory.

Fire marshals checked for incendiary devices in the theater after they received an anonymous warning.

· ·

1. just begun; in an initial or early stage of development, incipient.
2. not yet fully formed, undeveloped, incomplete.

During the inchoate stage of fetal growth, it is difficult to distinguish between a cow, a frog, or a human; as they mature, the developing embryos take on the characteristics of their own particular species.

INCOGNITO
(in·kog·née·toh) adj.

· ·

INCONTROVERTIBLE
(in·kon·trŏ·'vur·tĭ·běl) adj. or adv.

· ·

INCREDULOUS
(in·'krej·ŭ·lŭs) adj.

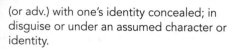

(or adv.) with one's identity concealed; in disguise or under an assumed character or identity.

The star was traveling incognito, hoping to find some measure of privacy on her vacation.

. . . .

indisputable, undeniable.

The photographs showed Brad and Allison together—their relationship was an incontrovertible fact.

. . . .

skeptical, unwilling to believe.

The members of the jury were incredulous when they heard the defendant's far-fetched explanation of the crime.

INCULCATE
(in·'kul·kayt) v.

· ·

INCURSION
(in·'kur·zhŏn) n.

· ·

INDEFATIGABLE
(in·di·'fat·ĭ·gă·bĕl) adj.

to teach and impress by frequent instruction or repetition; to indoctrinate, instill.

My parents worked hard to inculcate in me a deep sense of responsibility to others.

. . . .

a raid or temporary invasion of someone else's territory; the act of entering or running into a territory or domain.

There was an incursion on the western border of their country.

. . . .

not easily exhausted or fatigued; tireless.

The indefatigable volunteers worked until every piece of trash was removed from the beach.

INDOLENT
('in·dŏ·lĕnt) adj.

. . . .

INDOMITABLE
(in·'dom·i·tă·bĕl) adj.

. . . .

INELUCTABLE
(in·i·'luk·tă·bĕl) adj.

1. lazy, lethargic, inclined to avoid labor.
2. causing little or no pain; slow to grow or heal.

The construction foreman was hesitant to hire Earl because of his reputation of being indolent.

. . . .

not able to be vanquished or overcome, unconquerable; not easily discouraged or subdued.

The indomitable spirit of the Olympic athletes was inspirational.

. . . .

certain, inevitable; not to be avoided or overcome.

The ineluctable outcome of the two-person race was that there would be one winner and one loser.

INEPT
(in·'ept) adj.

. . . .

INFIDEL
('in·fi·děl) n.

. . . .

INGENUOUS
(in·'jen·yoo·ŭs) adj.

1. not suitable, inappropriate.
2. absurd, foolish.
3. incompetent, bungling and clumsy.

Trying to carry all of her suitcases at once was an inept way for Amanda to save time.

. . . .

1. a person with no religious beliefs.
2. a nonbeliever, one who does not accept a particular religion, doctrine, or system of beliefs.

Because he did not subscribe to the beliefs of the party, the members considered him an infidel.

. . . .

1. not cunning or deceitful, unable to mask feelings; artless, frank, sincere.
2. lacking sophistication or worldliness.

Don's expression of regret was ingenuous, for even though he didn't know her well, he felt a deep sadness when Mary died.

INIMITABLE
(i·'nim·i·tă·běl) adj.

· ·

INSCRUTABLE
(in·'scroo·tă·běl) adj.

· ·

INSOLENT
('in·sŏ·lěnt) adj.

defying imitation, unmatchable.

His performance on the tennis court was inimitable, and he won three championships.

. . . .

baffling, unfathomable, incapable of being understood.

It was completely inscrutable how the escape artist got out of the trunk.

. . . .

haughty and contemptuous; brazen, disrespectful, impertinent.

Parents of teenagers often observe the insolent behavior that typically accompanies adolescence.

INSOUCIANT
(in·'soo·see·ănt) adj.

. . . .

INTERDICT
(in·tĕr·'dikt) v.

. . . .

INTRACTABLE
(in·'trak·tă·běl) adj.

blithely unconcerned or carefree; nonchalant, indifferent.

Julian's insouciant attitude toward his finances will get him in trouble someday.

. . . .

to prohibit, forbid.

Carlos argued that the agriculture department should interdict plans to produce genetically modified foods.

. . . .

unmanageable, unruly, stubborn.

The intractable young colt proved difficult to train.

INTRANSIGENT
(in·'tran·si·jĕnt) adj.

....

INTREPID
(in·'trep·id) adj.

....

INURED
(in·'yoord) adj.

unwilling to compromise, stubborn.

Young children can be intransigent when it comes to what foods they will eat, insisting on familiar favorites and rejecting anything new.

. . . .

fearless, brave, undaunted.

Hunger had made the caveman intrepid, and he faced the mammoth without fear.

. . . .

accustomed to or adapted to something unpleasant.

Trisha had become inured to her boss's criticism, and it no longer bothered her.

INVEIGLE
(in·'vay·gĕl) v.

. . . .

INVETERATE
(in·'vet·ĕ·rit) adj.

. . . .

INVOLUTE
('in·vŏ·loot) adj.

to influence or persuade through gentle coaxing or flattery; to entice.

Vanessa inveigled her way into a promotion that should have gone to Maxon.

. . . .

habitual; deep rooted, firmly established.

I am an inveterate pacifist and am unlikely to change my mind.

. . . .

intricate, complex.

The tax reform committee faces an extremely involute problem if it wants to distribute the tax burden equally.

IOTA
(ī·'oh·tă) n.

. . . .

IRASCIBLE
(i·'ras·ĭ·běl) adj.

. . . .

IRE
(īr) n.

a very small amount; the smallest possible quantity.

Professor Carlton is so unpopular because he doesn't have one iota of respect for his students.

. . . .

irritable, easily aroused to anger, hot tempered.

Her irascible temperament caused many problems with the staff at the office.

. . . .

anger, wrath.

I was filled with ire when Vladimir tried to take credit for my work.

IRK
(urk) v.

. . . .

IRRESOLUTE
(i·'rez·ŏ·loot) adj.

. . . .

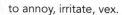

to annoy, irritate, vex.

*Being a teenager means being continually
irked by your parents—and vice versa.*

· ·

feeling or showing uncertainty; hesitant,
indecisive.

*Sandra is still irresolute, so if you talk to her
you might help her make up her mind.*

· ·

JARGON
('jahr·gǒn) n.

. . . .

JEJUNE
(ji·'joon) adj.

. . . .

JOCUND
('jok·ǔnd) adj.

J

1. specialized or technical language of a specific trade or group.
2. nonsensical or meaningless talk.

The technical manual was full of a lot of computer jargon.

. . . .

lacking substance, meager; hence: (a) lacking in interest or significance; insipid or dull (b) lacking in maturity, childish (c) lacking nutritional value.

The movie's trite and overly contrived plot make it a jejune sequel to what was a powerful and novel film.

. . . .

merry, cheerful; sprightly and lighthearted.

Alexi's jocund nature makes it a pleasure to be near her.

JUGGERNAUT

('jug·ĕr·nawt) n.

. . . .

J

1. a massive, overwhelmingly powerful and unstoppable force that seems to crush everything in its path.
2. Juggernaut, title for the Hindu god Krishna.

A shroud of fear covered Eastern Europe as the juggernaut of communism spread from nation to nation.

. . . .

LACONIC
(lă·'kon·ik) adj.

. . . .

LAISSEZ-FAIRE
(les·ay 'fair) adj.

. . . .

LANGUISH
('lang·gwish) v.

brief and to the point; succinct, terse, concise, often to the point of being curt or brusque.

Zse's laconic reply made it clear that he did not want to discuss the matter any further.

. . . .

hands-off; noninvolvement by the government in business and economic affairs.

Raheeb's laissez-faire management style is not only popular with our employees but also very successful—employee satisfaction is high, and profits are up for the third quarter in a row.

. . . .

1. to lose vigor or strength; to become languid, feeble, weak.
2. to exist or continue in a miserable or neglected state.

Lucinda languished in despair when Sven told her he'd fallen in love with another woman.

LATENT
('lay·tĕnt) adj.

. . . .

LAX
(laks) adj.

. . . .

LIAISON
(lee·'ay·zon, 'lee·ă·zon) n.

present or in existence but not active or evident.

Julian's latent musical talent surfaced when his parents bought an old piano at a garage sale and he learned to play it.

· ·

1. lacking in rigor or strictness; lenient.
2. not taut or rigid; flaccid, slack.

If parents are too lax with their toddlers, they may have a lot of trouble once they enter school, where children must follow a long list of rules and regulations.

· ·

1. a channel or means of connection or communication between two groups; one who maintains such communication.
2. a close relationship or link, especially one that is secretive or adulterous.

I have been elected to be the liaison between the union members and management.

LIBERTINE
('lib·ĕr·teen) n.

. . . .

LILLIPUTIAN
(lil·i·'pyoo·shăn) adj.

. . . .

LOQUACIOUS
(loh·'kway·shŭs) adj.

one who lives or acts in an immoral or irresponsible way; one who acts according to his or her own impulses and desires and is unrestrained by conventions or morals.

They claim to be avant-garde, but in my opinion, they're just a bunch of libertines.

. . . .

1. very small, tiny.
2. trivial or petty.

My troubles are lilliputian compared to hers, and I am thankful that I do not have such major issues in my life.

. . . .

talkative, garrulous.

The loquacious woman sitting next to me on the six-hour flight talked the entire time.

LUCID
('loo·sid) adj.

. . . .

LUCRATIVE
('loo·kră·tiv) adj.

. . . .

LUGUBRIOUS
(luu·'goo·bree·ŭs) adj.

L

1. very clear, easy to understand, intelligible.
2. sane or rational.

Andrea presented a very lucid argument that proved her point beyond a shadow of a doubt.

. . . .

profitable, producing much money.

A career as a teacher may not be lucrative, but it is rewarding.

. . . .

excessively dismal or mournful, often exaggeratedly or ridiculously so.

Irina's lugubrious tears made me believe that her sadness was just a façade.

MACHINATION
(mak·ĭ·ˈnay·shŏn) n.

. . . .

MAIM
(maym) v.

. . . .

MALADROIT
(mal·ă·ˈdroit) adj.

M

1. the act of plotting or devising.
2. a crafty or cunning scheme devised to achieve a sinister end.

Macbeth's machinations failed to bring him the glory he coveted, and only brought him tragedy.

. . . .

to wound, cripple, or injure, especially by depriving of the use of a limb or other part of the body; to mutilate, disfigure, disable.

The mining accident severely maimed Antol, and he was confined to a wheelchair.

. . . .

clumsy, bungling, inept.

The maladroit waiter broke a dozen plates and spilled coffee on two customers.

MALAISE
(mă·'layz) n.

. . . .

MALAPROPISM
('mal·ă·prop·iz·ĕm) n.

. . . .

MALFEASANCE
(măl·'fee·zăns) n.

a feeling of illness or unease.

After several tests, Wella finally learned the cause of her malaise: she was allergic to her new Siamese cat.

• •

comical misuse of words, especially those that are similar in sound.

His malapropisms when he speaks may make us laugh, but they won't win our vote.

• •

misconduct or wrongdoing, especially by a public official; improper professional conduct.

The city comptroller was found guilty of malfeasance, and he was removed from office.

MALINGER
(mǎ·'ling·gěr) v.

. . . .

MALLEABLE
('mal·ee·ǎ·běl) adj.

. . . .

MAR
(mahr) v.

M

M

to pretend to be injured or ill in order to avoid work.

Stop malingering and give me a hand with this job.

. . . .

1. easily molded or pressed into shape.
2. easily controlled or influenced.
3. easily adapting to changing circumstances.

You should be able to convince Xiu quickly—she's quite a malleable person.

. . . .

1. to impair or damage, make defective or imperfect.
2. to spoil the perfection or integrity of.

Omar's abysmal saxophone playing marred the serenity of the afternoon.

MAVERICK
('mav·ĕr·ik) n.

· ·

MEANDER
(mee·'an·dĕr) v.

· ·

MÉLANGE
(may·'lahnzh) n.

M

rebel, nonconformist, one who acts independently.

Madonna has always been a maverick in the music industry.

. . . .

1. to move on a winding or turning course.
2. to wander about, move aimlessly or without a fixed direction or course.

I meandered lost through the park for hours, trying to figure out how I could have made such an egregious mistake.

. . . .

a mixture or assortment.

The mélange of people at the party made for a scintillating evening.

MELLIFLUOUS
(me·'lif·loo·ŭs) adj.

. . . .

MENDACITY
(men·'das·i·tee) n.

. . . .

MERCURIAL
(měr·'kyoor·ee·ăl) adj.

sounding sweet and flowing; honeyed.

Her mellifluous voice floated in through the windows and made everyone smile.

· ·

1. the tendency to be dishonest or untruthful.
2. a falsehood or lie.

Carlos's mendacity has made him very unpopular with his classmates, who don't feel they can trust him.

· ·

1. liable to change moods suddenly.
2. lively, changeable, volatile.

Fiona is so mercurial that you never know what kind of reaction to expect.

MERETRICIOUS
(mer·'trish·ŭs) adj.

. . . .

METE
(meet) v.

. . . .

METICULOUS
(mĕ·'tik·yŭ·lŭs) adj.

gaudy, tawdry; showily attractive but false or insincere.

With its casinos and tacky attractions, some people consider Las Vegas the most meretricious city in the country.

• •

to distribute, allot, apportion.

The punishments were meted out fairly to everyone involved in the plot.

• •

extremely careful and precise; paying great attention to detail.

Tibor was awed by the meticulous detail in the painting—it looked as real as a photograph.

METTLESOME
('met·ĕl·sŏm) adj.

. . . .

MILIEU
(meel·'yuu) n.

. . . .

MINCE
(mins) v.

courageous, high-spirited.

Alice's mettlesome attitude was infectious and inspired us all to press on.

. . . .

environment or setting.

The milieu at the writer's retreat is designed to inspire creativity.

. . . .

1. to cut into very small pieces.
2. to walk or speak affectedly, as with studied refinement.
3. to say something more delicately or indirectly for the sake of politeness or decorum.

Please don't mince your words—just tell me what you want to say.

MINUTIAE
(mī·nōō'shēa) n., pl.

. . . .

MIRTH
(murth) n.

. . . .

MISANTHROPE
('mis·an·throhp) n.

very small details; trivial or trifling matters.

His attention to the minutiae of the process enabled him to make his great discovery.

· ·

great merriment, joyous laughter.

The wedding celebration filled the reception hall with mirth throughout the evening.

· ·

one who hates or distrusts humankind.

He's a real misanthrope, and no one can do anything right in his eyes.

MISCREANT
('mis·kree·ănt) n.

. . . .

MITIGATE
('mit·ĭ·gayt) v.

. . . .

MOLLIFY
('mol·ĭ·fī) v.

a villain, criminal; evil person.

The miscreant had eluded police for months, but today he was finally captured.

· ·

1. to make less intense or severe.
2. to moderate the force or intensity of, soften, diminish, alleviate.

I am sure that if you tell the headmaster the truth, the extenuating circumstances will mitigate the severity of your punishment.

· ·

1. to soothe the anger of, calm.
2. to lessen in intensity.
3. to soften, make less rigid.

The crying child was quickly mollified by her mother's comforting voice.

MOOT
(moot) adj.

. . . .

MOROSE
(mŏ·'rohs) adj.

. . . .

MULTIFARIOUS
(mul·ti·'fair·ee·ŭs) adj.

M

debatable, undecided; nor worth discussion.

Although this is a moot issue, it is one that is still argued about among certain circles.

. . . .

gloomy, sullen, melancholy.

My daughter has been morose ever since our dog ran away.

. . . .

very varied, greatly diversified; having many aspects.

The job requires the ability to handle multifarious tasks.

MUNDANE
(mun·'dayn) adj.

. . . .

MYRIAD
('mir·ee·ăd) adj.

. . . .

M

1. ordinary, commonplace, dull.
2. worldly, secular, not spiritual.

If you do not have passion for your job, going to work each day can become mundane.

. . . .

too numerous to be counted; innumerable.

n. an indefinitely large number; an immense number, vast amount.

To the refugees from Somalia, the myriad choices in the American supermarket were overwhelming.

. . . .

NADIR
('nay·dĭr) n.

. . . .

NARCISSISM
('narh·si·siz·ĕm) n.

. . . .

NASCENT
('nas·ĕnt) adj.

the very bottom, the lowest point.

When he felt he was at the nadir of his life, Robert began to practice mediation to elevate his spirits.

. . . .

admiration or worship of oneself; excessive interest in one's own personal features.

Some critics say movie stars are guilty of narcissism.

. . . .

coming into existence, emerging.

The nascent movement gathered strength quickly and soon became a nationwide call to action.

NEMESIS
('nem·ĕ·sis) n.

. . . .

NEXUS
('nek·sŭs) n.

. . . .

NOISOME
('noi·sŏm) adj.

1. source of harm or ruin, the cause of one's misery or downfall; bane.
2. agent of retribution or vengeance.

In Frankenstein, *the monster Victor creates becomes his nemesis.*

. . . .

1. a means of connection, a link or tie between a series of things.
2. a connected series or group.
3. the core or center.

The nexus between the lobbyists and the recent policy changes is clear.

. . . .

1. offensive, foul, especially in odor; putrid.
2. harmful, noxious.

What a noisome odor is coming from that garbage can!

NON SEQUITUR
(non 'sek·wi·tŭr) n.

. . . .

NONCHALANT
(non·shă·'lahnt) adj.

. . . .

NOVEL
('nov·ĕl) n.

a conclusion that does not logically follow from the evidence.

Marcus's argument started off strong, but it degenerated into a series of non sequiturs.

• •

indifferent or cool, not showing anxiety or excitement.

Victoria tried to be nonchalant, but I could tell she was nervous.

• •

a genre of literature.
adj. strikingly new, original, or different.

The chef's novel idea to add mango to the salad was a hit with patrons.

NOXIOUS
('nok·shŭs) adj.

. . . .

NULLIFY
('nul·ĭ·fī) v.

. . . .

unpleasant and harmful, unwholesome.

The noxious smell drove everyone from the room.

. . . .

1. to make null (without legal force), invalidate.
2. to counteract or neutralize the effect of.

The opponents wanted to nullify the bill before it became a law.

. . . .

OBDURATE
('ob·dŭ·rit) adj.

· ·

OBFUSCATE
(ob·'fus·kayt) v.

· ·

OBSEQUIOUS
(ŏb·'see·kwee·ŭs) adj.

stubborn and inflexible; hardhearted, not easily moved to pity.

I doubt he'll change his mind; he's the most obdurate person I know.

. . . .

1. to make obscure or unclear, to muddle or make difficult to understand.
2. to dim or darken.

Instead of clarifying the matter, Walter only obfuscated it further.

. . . .

excessively or ingratiatingly compliant or submissive; attentive in a servile or ingratiating manner, fawning.

The obsequious manner of the butler made it clear that he resented his position.

OBSTREPEROUS
(ob·'strep·ĕ·rŭs) adj.

. . . .

OBTRUSIVE
(ŏb·'troo·siv) adj.

. . . .

OBTUSE
(ŏb·'toos) adj.

noisily and stubbornly defiant; aggressively
boisterous, unruly.

The obstreperous child refused to go to bed.

. . . .

1. prominent, undesirably noticeable.
2. projecting, thrusting out.
3. tending to push one's self or one's ideas
upon others, forward, intrusive.

*Minsun survived the accident, but she was left
with several obtrusive scars.*

. . . .

1. stupid and slow to understand.
2. blunt, not sharp or pointed.

*Please don't be so obtuse—you know what I
mean.*

OBVIATE
('ob·vee·ayt) v.

. . . .

OCCULT
(ŏ·'kult) adj.

. . . .

ODIOUS
('oh·di·ŭs) adj.

to make unnecessary, get rid of.

Hiring Magdalena as a housekeeper will obviate the need to hire a music tutor, for she is also a classical pianist.

. . . .

1. secret, hidden, concealed.
2. involving the realm of the supernatural.
3. beyond ordinary understanding, incomprehensible.

The embezzler was good at keeping his financial records occult from the authorities.

. . . .

contemptible, hateful, detestable.

Zachary found the work in the slaughterhouse so odious that he quit after one day and became a vegetarian.

OEUVRE
('uu·vrĕ) n.

. . . .

OFFICIOUS
(ŏ·'fish·ŭs) adj.

. . . .

OLIGARCHY
('ol·ĭ·gahr·kee) n.

O

1. a work of art.
2. the total lifework of a writer, artist, composer, etc.

Constanta's latest addition to his oeuvre is an avant-garde symphony featuring a cow bell solo.

. . . .

meddlesome, bossy; eagerly offering unnecessary or unwanted advice.

My officious Aunt Midge is coming to the party, so be prepared for lots of questions and advice.

. . . .

form of government in which the power is in the hands of a select few.

The small governing body calls itself a democracy, but it is clearly an oligarchy.

OMNIPOTENT
(om·'nip·ŏ·tĕnt) adj.

. . . .

OMNISCIENT
(om·'nish·ĕnt) adj.

. . . .

ONUS
('oh·nŭs) n.

having unlimited or universal power or force.

In Greek mythology, Zeus was the most powerful god, but he was not omnipotent: his rule was often held in check by the unchangeable laws of the Three Fates.

· ·

having infinite knowledge; knowing all things.

In a story with an omniscient narrator, we can hear the thoughts and feelings of all of the characters.

· ·

duty or responsibility of doing something; task, burden.

It was Clark's idea, so the onus was on him to show us that it would work.

OPPROBRIOUS
(ŏ·'proh·bree·ŭs) adj.

. . . .

OPULENT
('op·yŭ·lĕnt) adj.

. . . .

OSCILLATE
('os·ĭ·layt) v.

1. expressing contempt or reproach; scornful, abusive.
2. bringing shame or disgrace.

It was inappropriate to make such opprobrious remarks in front of everybody.

. . . .

1. possessing great wealth, affluent.
2. abundant, luxurious.

Lee does not live an opulent lifestyle despite having a well-paying job.

. . . .

1. to swing back and forth or side to side in a steady, uninterrupted rhythm.
2. to waver, as between two conflicting options or opinions; vacillate.

The rhythm of the oscillating fan put the baby to sleep.

OSTENSIBLE
(o·'sten·sĭ·bĕl) adj.

. . . .

OSTRACIZE
('os·tră ·sīz) v.

. . . .

OVERWEENING
(oh·vĕr·'wee·ning) adj.

seeming, appearing as such, put forward (as of a reason) but not necessarily so; pretended.

The ostensible reason for the meeting is to discuss the candidates, but I believe they have already made their decision.

. . . .

to reject, cast out from a group or from society.

Kendall was ostracized after he repeatedly stole from his friends.

. . . .

1. presumptuously arrogant, overbearing.
2. excessive, immoderate.

I quit because I couldn't stand to work for such an overweening boss.

OXYMORON
(oks·ee·'moh·rŏn) n.

. . . .

a figure of speech containing a seemingly contradictory combination of expressions, such as friendly fire.

The term "nonworking mother" is a contemptible oxymoron.

. . . .

PALLIATE
('pal·ee·ayt) v.

. . . .

PALLOR
('pal·ŏr) n.

. . . .

PALTRY
('pawl·tree) adj.

P

1. to make something less intense or severe, mitigate, alleviate; to gloss over, put a positive spin on.
2. to provide relief from pain, relieve the symptoms of a disease or disorder.

The governor tried to palliate his malfeasance, but it soon became clear that he would not be able to prevent a scandal.

. . . .

paleness, lack of color.

The fever subsided, but her pallor remained for several weeks.

. . . .

1. lacking in importance or worth, insignificant; contemptibly small in amount.
2. wretched or contemptible, pitiful.

Walton couldn't believe the billionaire offered such a paltry reward for the return of his lost dog.

PARADIGM
('par·ă·dĭm) n.

. . . .

PAR EXCELLENCE
(pahr 'ek·sĕ·lahns) adj.

. . . .

PARIAH
(pă·'rī·ă) n.

1. something that serves as a model or example.
2. set of assumptions, beliefs, values or practices that constitutes a way of understanding or doing things.

Elected "Employee of the Month," Winona is a paradigm of efficiency.

. . . .

being the best or truest of its kind, quintessential; having the highest degree of excellence, beyond comparison.

Bob Hope was an entertainer par excellence.

. . . .

an outcast, a rejected and despised person.

After he told a sexist joke, Jason was treated like a pariah by all of the women in the office.

PARTISAN
('pahr·ti·zăn) n.

. . . .

PAUCITY
('paw·si·tee) n.

. . . .

PARVENU
('pahr·vě·noo) n.

1. a person fervently and often uncritically supporting a group or cause.
2. a guerilla, a member of an organized body of fighters who attack or harass an enemy.

The partisan lobby could not see the logic of the opposing senator's argument, and did not understand how the proposed legislation would infringe upon basic constitutional rights.

. . . .

scarcity, smallness of supply or quantity.

The paucity of food in the area drove the herd farther and farther to the south.

. . . .

a person who has suddenly risen to a higher social or economic status but has not been socially accepted by others in that class; an upstart.

Because he was "new money" in an "old money" town, Rodney was a parvenu who struggled to be accepted by his wealthy peers.

PECCADILLO
(pek·ă·'dil·oh) n.

. . . .

PECUNIARY
(pi·'kyoo·nee·er·ee) adj.

. . . .

PEDANTIC
(pi·'dăn·tik) n.

TOEFL iBT® VOCABULARY FLASH REVIEW

a trivial offense, a small sin or fault.

Don't make such a big deal out of a little peccadillo.

. . . .

of, relating to, or involving money.

Rosen was relieved to learn that his penalty would be pecuniary only and that he would not have to spend any time in jail.

. . . .

adj. marked by a narrow, tiresome focus on or display of learning, especially of rules or trivial matters.

Her lessons were so pedantic that I found I was easily bored.

PEDESTRIAN
(pě·'des·tri· ăn) n.

. . . .

PELLUCID
(pě·'loo·sid) adj.

. . . .

PENCHANT
('pen·chănt) n.

a walker.

adj. commonplace, trite;
unremarkable, unimaginative, dull.

*Although the film received critical acclaim, its
pedestrian plot has been overused by
screenwriters for decades.*

. . . .

1. translucent, able to be seen through with
clarity.
2. (e.g., of writing) very clear, easy to
understand.

*Senator Waterson's pellucid argument made
me change my vote.*

. . . .

a strong liking or inclination (for something).

*Consuela has a penchant for wearing the latest
fashions.*

PENSIVE
('pen·siv) adj.

. . . .

PENULTIMATE
(pi·'nul·tī·mit) adj.

. . . .

PENURY
('pen·yŭ·ree) n.

deeply thoughtful, especially in a serious or melancholy manner.

After the terrible car accident, Anoki was pensive about what he should do with his life.

. . . .

next to last.

There's a real surprise for the audience in the penultimate scene.

. . . .

extreme poverty, destitution.

After ten years of penury, it's good to be financially secure again.

PEREMPTORY
(pĕ·'remp·tŏ·ree) adj.

. . . .

PERFIDIOUS
(pĕr·'fid·ee·ŭs) adj.

. . . .

PERFUNCTORY
(pĕr·'fungk·tŏ·ree) adj.

P

1. offensively self-assured, dictatorial.
2. commanding, imperative, not allowing contradiction or refusal.
3. putting an end to debate or action.

The mother's peremptory tone ended the children's bickering.

. . . .

treacherous, dishonest; violating good faith, disloyal.

The perfidious knight betrayed his king.

. . . .

done out of a sense of duty or routine but without much care or interest; superficial, not thorough.

We were not satisfied with his perfunctory work; we felt a more thorough job could have been done.

PERJURY
('pur·jŭ·ree) n.

. . . .

PERNICIOUS
(pĕr·'nish·u˘s) adj.

. . . .

PERSONABLE
('pur·sŏ·nă·bĕl) adj.

the deliberate giving of false, misleading, or incomplete testimony while under oath.

William was convicted of perjury for lying about his whereabouts on the night of the crime.

. . . .

deadly, harmful, very destructive.

Nancy's opponent started a pernicious rumor that destroyed her chances of winning.

. . . .

pleasing in appearance or manner, attractive.

Sandra is personable and well liked by her peers.

PERTINACIOUS
(pur·tĭ·'nay·shŭs) adj.

. . . .

PERVADE
(pĕr·'vayd) v.

. . . .

PETRIFY
('pet·rĭ·fī) v.

extremely stubborn or persistent; holding firmly to a belief, purpose, or course of action.

The pertinacious journalist finally uncovered the truth about the factory's illegal disposal of toxins.

. . . .

to spread everywhere, permeate; to be diffused or present throughout.

Fear pervaded the classroom after Sally started a rumor that Mr. Higgins would be their new teacher.

. . . .

1. to make hard or stiff like a stone.
2. to stun or paralyze with fear, astonishment, or dread.

I was petrified when I heard the door open in the middle of the night.

PETULANT
('pech·ŭ·lănt) adj.

. . . .

PHILISTINE
('fil·i·steen) n.

. . . .

PHOENIX
('fee·niks) n.

P

peevish; unreasonably or easily irritated or annoyed.

The sulking child could only be described as petulant.

. . . .

a smug, ignorant person unconcerned with art or culture; someone who is uncultured and commonplace.

Richards thinks he is cosmopolitan, but he's really just a philistine.

. . . .

1. a person or thing of unmatched beauty or excellence.
2. a person or thing that has become renewed or restored after suffering calamity or apparent annihilation (after the mythological bird that periodically immolated itself and rose from the ashes as a new phoenix).

The phoenix is often used to symbolize something that is indomitable or immortal.

PILLAGE
('pil·ij) v.

. . . .

PIQUANT
('pee·kănt) adj.

. . . .

PIQUE
(peek) v.

to forcibly rob of goods, especially in time of war; to plunder.

The barbarians pillaged the village before destroying it with fire.

. . . .

1. agreeably pungent, sharp or tart in taste.
2. pleasantly stimulating or provocative.

The spicy shrimp salad is wonderfully piquant.

. . . .

1. to wound (someone's) pride, to offend.
2. to arouse or provoke.

The article really piqued my interest in wildlife preservation.

PITH
(pith) n.

. . . .

PIVOTAL
('piv·ŏ·tăl) adj.

. . . .

PLACID
('plas·id) adj.

P

1. the essential or central part; the heart or essence (of the matter, idea, experience, etc.).
2. (in biology) the soft, spongelike central cylinder of the stems of most flowering plants.

Her concise statement went right to the pith of the argument and covered the most important issues.

· ·

being of vital importance, crucial.

We are at a pivotal point in the negotiations and must proceed very carefully; the wrong move now could ruin everything.

· ·

calm and peaceful; free from disturbance or tumult.

Lake Placid is as calm and peaceful as its name suggests.

TOEFL iBT® VOCABULARY FLASH REVIEW

PLAINTIVE
('playn·tiv) adj.

. . . .

PLATITUDE
('plat·i·tood) n.

. . . .

PLETHORA
('pleth·ŏ·rǎ) n.

expressing sorrow; mournful, melancholy.

Janice's plaintive voice made me decide to stay and comfort her longer.

. . . .

a trite or banal statement, especially one uttered as if it were new.

Matthew offered me several platitudes but no real advice.

. . . .

an overabundance, extreme excess.

There was a plethora of food options at the reception.

POIGNANT
('poin·yănt) adj.

· ·

POLEMICAL
(pŏ ·'lem·ik·ăl) adj.

· ·

POSEUR
(poh·'zur) n.

1. arousing emotion, deeply moving, touching.
2. keenly distressing; piercing or incisive.

They captured the poignant reunion on film.

. . . .

controversial, argumentative.

The analyst presented a highly polemical view of the economic situation.

. . . .

someone who takes on airs to impress others; a phony.

My first impression of the arrogant newcomer told me he was a poseur—I had a hunch he wasn't what he seemed to be.

PRAGMATIC
(prag·'mat·ik) adj.

. . . .

PRECARIOUS
(pri·'kair·ee·ŭs) adj.

. . . .

PRECEPT
('pree·sept) n.

P

practical, matter-of-fact; favoring utility.

Because we don't have money or time to waste, I think we should take the most pragmatic approach.

. . . .

1. fraught with danger.
2. dangerously unsteady or insecure.

The crocodile hunter is constantly placing himself in very precarious positions.

. . . .

a rule establishing standards of conduct.

The headmaster reviewed the precepts of the school with the students.

TOEFL iBT® VOCABULARY FLASH REVIEW

PRECIPITOUS
(pri·'sip·i·tŭs) adj.

. . . .

PRETENTIOUS
(pri·'ten·shŭs) adj.

. . . .

PREVARICATE
(pri·'var·ĭ·kayt) v.

1. extremely steep, dropping sharply.
2. hasty, rash, foolhardy.

Driving through the state park, we spotted a grizzly bear on a precipitous cliff and wondered if he would fall.

. . . .

showy, pompous, putting on airs.

Hannah thinks that being pretentious will make people like her, but she is sorely mistaken.

. . . .

to tell lies, to stray from or evade the truth.

Quit prevaricating and tell me what really happened.

PRIMEVAL
(prī·'mee·văl) adj.

. . . .

PRISTINE
('pris·teen) adj.

. . . .

PRODIGAL
('prod·ĭ·găl) adj.

ancient, original, belonging to the earliest ages.

The primeval art found in the caves was discovered by accident.

. . . .

1. in its original and unspoiled condition, unadulterated.
2. clean, pure; free from contamination.

We were awed by the beauty of the pristine forest in northern Canada.

. . . .

1. recklessly wasteful or extravagant, especially with money.
2. given in great abundance, lavish or profuse.

His prodigal actions led to his financial ruin.

PROFLIGATE
('prof·lĭ·git) adj.

· ·

PROLETARIAT
(proh·lĕ·'tair·ee·ăt) n.

· ·

PROPINQUITY
(proh·'ping·kwi·tee) n.

1. recklessly wasteful or extravagant, prodigal.
2. lacking moral restraint, dissolute.

The profligate man quickly depleted his fortune.

· ·

the working class; those who do manual labor to earn a living.

The proletariat demanded fewer hours and better wages.

· ·

1. proximity, nearness.
2. affinity, similarity in nature.

The propinquity of these two mineral elements makes them difficult to tell apart.

PROPITIOUS
(proh·'pish·ŭs) adj.

. . . .

PROSAIC
(proh·'zay·ik) adj.

. . . .

PROSCRIBE
(proh·'skrīb) v.

auspicious, presenting favorable circumstances.

These are propitious omens and foretell a good journey.

. . . .

unimaginative, ordinary, dull.

The prosaic novel was rejected by the publisher.

. . . .

1. to prohibit, forbid; to banish or outlaw.
2. to denounce or condemn.

The king proscribed the worship of idols in his kingdom, and decreed there was only one God.

PROSELYTIZE
('pros·ĕ·li·tīz) v.

. . . .

PROTEAN
('proh·tee·ăn) adj.

. . . .

PROTOCOL
('proh·tŏ·kawl) n.

to convert or seek to convert someone to another religion, belief, doctrine, or cause.

After a few minutes, it became clear to Hannah that the purpose of the meeting was really to proselytize as many attendees as possible.

· ·

taking many forms, changeable; variable, versatile.

In Native American mythology, the coyote is often called the "shape shifter" because he is such a protean character.

· ·

1. etiquette, ceremony, or procedure with regard to people's rank or status.
2. a first copy of a treaty or document.

Jackson was fired for repeatedly refusing to follow protocol.

PROVIDENT
('prov·i·děnt) adj.

. . . .

PROXY
('prok·see) n.

. . . .

PRUDENT
('proo·děnt) adj.

wisely providing for future needs; frugal, economical.

Because my parents were so provident, I didn't have to struggle to pay for college.

. . . .

1. a person or agent authorized to represent or act for another.
2. a document authorizing this substitution.

The president appointed a proxy to handle business matters during his absence.

. . . .

careful and sensible regarding one's actions and interests; exercising good judgment, judicious.

Clarissa has always been very prudent, so her recent bout of poor choices and boisterous behavior tells me she is very upset about something.

PUERILE
('pyoŏ·rĭl) adj.

· ·

PUGNACIOUS
(pug·'nay·shŭs) adj.

· ·

PUNCTILIOUS
(pungk·'til·i·ŭs) adj.

1. childish, immature.
2. suitable only for children, belonging to or of childhood.

Andrew is a remarkably successful business-man for someone so puerile.

. . . .

contentious, quarrelsome, eager to fight, belligerent.

Don't be so pugnacious—I don't want to fight you.

. . . .

extremely attentive to detail, very meticulous and precise.

One of the reasons he excels as an editor is because he is so punctilious.

PUNDIT
('pun·dit) n.

. . . .

PUNGENT
('pun·jĕnt) adj.

. . . .

PURGE
(purj) v.

P

a learned person or scholar; one who is an authority on a subject.

The journalist consulted several legal pundits before drafting the article.

. . . .

1. having a strong, sharp taste or smell.
2. penetrating, caustic, stinging.

Some people may find it to be too much, but I enjoy a pungent curry.

. . . .

to free from impurities, especially to rid of that which is undesirable or harmful; to make or become clean, pure.

After Leon writes a draft, he purges the text of unnecessary words to make it more succinct.

PURLOIN
(pŭr·'loin) v.

. . . .

PURPORT
('pur·pohrt) v.

. . . .

to steal.

The thief purloined a sculpture worth thousands of dollars.

. . . .

1. to be intended to seem, to have the appearance of being.
2. propose or intend.

The letter purports to express your opinion on the matter, however you've said different things in person.

. . . .

QUAFF
(kwahf) v.

. . . .

QUAIL
(kwayl) v.

. . . .

QUERULOUS
('kwer·ŭ·lŭs) adj.

to drink hurriedly or heartily; to swallow in large draughts.

He quickly quaffed three glasses of water.

. . . .

to draw back in fear, flinch, cower.

Mona quailed as soon as the vicious dog entered the room.

. . . .

complaining, peevish, discontented.

He's a cantankerous and querulous old man, but I love him.

QUEUE
(kyoo) n.

. . . .

QUID PRO QUO
(kwid proh 'kwoh) n.

. . . .

QUIESCENT
(kwi·'es·ĕnt) adj.

1. a line of people or vehicles waiting their turn.
2. (in information processing) an ordered list of tasks to be performed or sequence of programs awaiting processing.

Look how long the queue is! We'll be waiting for hours.

. . . .

a thing given in return for something; an equal exchange or substitution.

I won't agree to any deal that isn't quid pro quo—it must be a win-win arrangement.

. . . .

inactive, quiet, at rest; dormant, latent.

The volcano is quiescent at the moment, but who knows when it will erupt again.

QUINTESSENCE
(kwin·'tes·ĕns) n.

. . . .

QUIXOTIC
(kwik·'sot·ik) adj.

. . . .

QUOTIDIAN
(kwoh·'tid·ee·ăn) adj.

1. the essence of a substance.
2. the perfect example or embodiment of something.

Maura is the quintessence of kindness.

. . . .

extravagantly chivalrous and unselfish; romantically idealistic, impractical.

His quixotic ways charmed all the women at the dance.

. . . .

1. daily.
2. commonplace, pedestrian.

Prudence took her quotidian dose of medicine.

RAKISH
('ray·kish) adj.

. . . .

RANCOR
('rang·kŏr) n.

. . . .

RAPACIOUS
(ră·'pay·shŭs) adj.

R

1. debonair, smartly dressed or mannered, jaunty in appearance or manner.
2. unconventional and disreputable; dissolute or debauched.

The rakish young man charmed everyone at the table.

· ·

a bitter feeling of ill will, long-lasting resentment.

Greg is full of rancor towards his brother, and this causes tension at family gatherings.

· ·

excessively greedy and grasping (especially for money); voracious, plundering.

The rapacious general ordered his soldiers to pillage the town and take everything of value.

RAUCOUS
('raw·kŭs) adj.

. . . .

REACTIONARY
(ree·'ak·shŏ·ner·ee) n.

. . . .

REBUKE
(ri·'byook) v.

1. unpleasantly loud and harsh.
2. boisterous, disorderly, disturbing the peace.

The raucous music kept us awake all night.

. . . .

a person who favors political conservativism;
one who is opposed to progress or liberalism.

*It should be an interesting marriage: he's a
reactionary, and she's as liberal as they come.*

. . . .

1. to criticize sharply; to reprove or reprimand,
censure.
2. to repress or restrain by expressing harsh
disapproval.

*After weeks of being rebuked in front of his
coworkers for minor infractions and imaginary
offenses, Ameer realized he was being
persecuted by his boss.*

TOEFL iBT® VOCABULARY FLASH REVIEW

RECALCITRANT
(ri·'kal·si·trănt) adj.

. . . .

RECIDIVISM
(ri·'sid·ĭ·vizm) n.

. . . .

RECONDITE
('rek·ŏn·dīt) adj.

disobedient, unruly, refusing to obey authority.

The recalcitrant child was sent to the principal's office for the third time in a week.

. . . .

a relapse or backslide, especially into antiso-cial or criminal behavior after conviction and punishment.

Allowing prisoners to earn their GED while incarcerated has been shown to greatly reduce recidivism and repeat offenses.

. . . .

1. not easily understood, obscure, abstruse.
2. dealing with abstruse or profound matters.

He loves the challenge of grasping a recondite subject.

RECONNOITER
(ree·kŏ·'noi·tĕr) v.

. . . .

REFRACTORY
(ri·'frak·tŏ·ree) adj.

. . . .

REGALE
(ri·'gayl) v.

to make a preliminary inspection or survey of, especially to gather military information or prepare for military operations.

My job was to reconnoiter the party and let my friends know if it was worth attending.

. . . .

stubborn, unmanageable, resisting control or discipline.

Elena is a counselor for refractory children in an alternative school setting.

. . . .

to delight or entertain with a splendid feast or pleasant amusement.

The king regaled his guests with music and storytellers until the early morning hours.

REMONSTRATE
(ri·'mon·strayt) v.

. . . .

RENDEZVOUS
('rahn·dĕ·voo) n.

. . . .

RENEGADE
('ren·ĕ·gayd) n.

1. to say or plead in protest, objection, or opposition.
2. to scold or reprove.

The children remonstrated loudly when their mother told them they couldn't watch the movie.

. . . .

1. a prearranged meeting at a certain time and place.
2. a place where people meet, especially a popular gathering place.
v. to bring or come together at a certain place, to meet at a rendezvous.

Clarissa and Ahmed planned a rendezvous in the park after lunch.

. . . .

1. a deserter; one who rejects a cause, group, etc.
2. a person who rebels and becomes an outlaw.

The renegade soldier decided to join the guerrilla fighters.

RENOWNED
(ri·'nownd) adj.

. . . .

REPARTEE
(rep·ăr·'tee) n.

. . . .

REPLETE
(ri·'pleet) adj.

famous; widely known and esteemed.

The renowned historian Stephen Ambrose wrote many books that were popular both with scholars and the general public.

· ·

1. a quick, witty reply.
2. the ability to make witty replies.

He wasn't expecting such a sharp repartee from someone who was normally so quiet.

· ·

1. well stocked or abundantly supplied.
2. full, gorged.

The house was replete with expensive antiques.

REPOSE
(ri·'pohz) n.

. . . .

REPREHENSIBLE
(rep·ri·'hen·sĭ·bĕl) adj.

. . . .

REPRIEVE
(ri·'preev) n.

1. resting or being at rest.
2. calmness, tranquility, peace of mind.

The wail of a police siren disturbed my repose.

. . . .

deserving rebuke or censure.

The reprehensible behavior of the neighborhood bully angered everyone on the block.

. . . .

1. postponement or cancellation of punishment, especially of the death sentence.
2. temporary relief from danger or discomfort.

The court granted him a reprieve at the last moment because of DNA evidence that absolved him of the crime.

REPRISAL
(ri·'prī·zăl) n.

. . . .

REPROBATE
('rep·ro˘·bayt) n.

. . . .

REPUDIATE
(ri·'pyoo·di·ayt) v.

1. an act of retaliation for an injury with the intent of inflicting at least as much harm in return.
2. the practice of using political or military force without actually resorting to war.

The president promised a swift reprisal for the attack.

. . . .

an immoral or unprincipled person; one without scruples.

Edgar deemed himself a reprobate, a criminal, and a traitor in his written confession.

. . . .

to disown, disavow, reject completely.

Mrs. Tallon has repeatedly repudiated your accusations.

RESCIND
(ri·'sind) v.

. . . .

RESONANT
('rez·ŏ·nănt) adj.

. . . .

RESPLENDENT
(ri·'splen·děnt) adj.

to repeal or cancel; to void or annul.

The Olsens rescinded their offer to buy the house when they discovered the property was in a flood zone.

· ·

echoing, resounding.

The new announcer at the stadium has a wonderfully resonant voice.

· ·

having great splendor or beauty; dazzling, brilliant.

Sanjay stood for a long time on the deck, watching a resplendent sunset over the mountains.

RETICENT
('ret·i·sĕnt) adj.

· ·

REVERE
(ri·'veer) v.

· ·

RIGMAROLE
('rig·mă·rohl) (also rigamarole) n.

tending to keep one's thoughts and feelings to oneself; reserved, untalkative, silent.

Annette is very reticent, so don't expect her to tell you much about herself.

. . . .

to regard with reverence or awe; to venerate, hold in highest respect or estimation.

When you look at Judith's work, it's easy to see which painter she reveres most: every painting is an homage to Cézanne.

. . . .

1. rambling, confusing, incoherent talk.
2. a complicated, petty procedure.

We had to go through a great deal of rigmarole to get this approved.

ROGUE
(rohg) n.

. . . .

ROIL
(roil) v.

. . . .

RUBRIC
('roo·brik) n.

1. a dishonest, unprincipled person.
2. a pleasantly mischievous person.
3. a vicious and solitary animal living apart from the herd.

Yesterday, that rogue hid all of my cooking utensils; today he's switched everything around in the cupboards!

. . . .

1. to make a liquid cloudy or muddy.
2. to stir up or agitate.
3. to anger or annoy.

The crowd was roiled by the speaker's insensitive remarks.

. . . .

1. a class or category.
2. a heading, title, or note of explanation or direction.

I would put this under the rubric of "quackery," not "alternative medicine."

SACRILEGIOUS
(sak·rǐ·'lij·ǔs) adj.

. . . .

SAGACIOUS
(sǎ·'gay·shǔs) adj.

. . . .

SALIENT
('say·lee·ěnt) adj.

disrespectful or irreverent towards something regarded as sacred.

Her book was criticized by the church for being sacrilegious.

. . . .

having or showing sound judgment; perceptive, wise.

My sagacious uncle always gives me good advice.

. . . .

1. conspicuous, prominent, highly noticeable; drawing attention through a striking quality.
2. springing up or jutting out.

Jill's most salient feature is her stunning auburn hair.

SALUTARY
('sal·yŭ·ter·ee) adj.

. . . .

SANCTIMONIOUS
(sangk·tĭ·'moh·nee·ŭs) adj.

. . . .

SANCTION
('sangk·shŏn) n.

TOEFL iBT® VOCABULARY FLASH REVIEW

producing a beneficial or wholesome effect; remedial.

To promote better health, I've decided to move to a more salutary climate.

. . . .

hypocritically pious or devout; excessively self-righteous.

The thief's sanctimonious remark that "a fool and his money are soon parted" only made the jury more eager to convict him.

. . . .

1. official authorization or approval.
2. a penalty imposed to coerce another to comply or conform.

v. to approve or permit; to give official authorization or approval for; to ratify.

The city council has sanctioned our request to turn the empty lot into a community garden.

SANGFROID
(sahn·'frwah) n.

· ·

SANGUINE
('sang·gwin) adj.

· ·

SARDONIC
(sahr·'don·ik) adj.

composure, especially in dangerous or difficult circumstances.

I wish I had Jane's sangfroid when I find myself in a confrontational situation.

1. confidently cheerful, optimistic.
2. of the color of blood; red.

People are drawn to her because of her sanguine and pleasant nature.

. . . .

sarcastic, mocking scornfully.

I was hurt by his sardonic reply.

TOEFL iBT® VOCABULARY FLASH REVIEW

SATURNINE
('sat·ŭr·nīn) adj.

. . . .

SAVOIR FAIRE
('sav·wahr 'fair) n.

. . . .

SCHISM
('siz·ĕm) n.

gloomy, dark, sullen.

The saturnine child sulked for hours.

• •

knowledge of the right thing to do or say in a social situation; graceful tact.

Adele's savoir faire makes her the quintessential hostess.

• •

a separation or division into factions because of a difference in belief or opinion.

The schism between the two parties was forgotten as they united around a common cause.

SCINTILLA
(sin·'til·ă) n.

. . . .

SCINTILLATING
('sin·tī·lay·ting) adj.

. . . .

SCURVY
('skur·vee) adj.

a trace or particle; minute amount, iota.

She has not one scintilla of doubt about his guilt.

. . . .

1. sparkling, shining brilliantly.
2. brilliantly clever and animated.

I had planned to leave the dinner party early, but the conversation was so scintillating that I stayed until two in the morning.

. . . .

contemptible, mean.

That scurvy knave has ruined my plans again.

SEDITIOUS
(si·'dish·ŭs) adj.

. . . .

SEDULOUS
('sej·ŭ·lŭs) adj.

. . . .

SEMANTICS
(si·'man·tiks) n.

arousing to insurrection or rebellion; engaging in or promoting sedition (conduct or language which incites resistance or opposition to lawful authority).

Toby's seditious behavior nearly started a riot at the town meeting.

. . . .

diligent, persevering, hard working.

After years of sedulous research, the scientists discovered a cure.

. . . .

1. the study of meaning in language.
2. the meaning, connotation, or interpretation of words, symbols, or other forms.
3. the study of relationships between signs or symbols and their meanings.

He claims it's an issue of semantics, but the matter is not open to interpretation.

SENTENTIOUS
(sen·'ten·shŭs) adj.

. . . .

SERVILE
('sur·vīl) adj.

. . . .

SHIFTLESS
('shift·lis) adj.

1. expressing oneself tersely, pithy.
2. full of maxims and proverbs offered in a self-righteous manner.

I was looking for your honest opinion, not a sententious reply.

. . . .

1. pertaining to or befitting a slave or forced labor.
2. abjectly submissive, slavish.

The climax comes when Yolanda, who had believed she was doomed to play the role of a servile wife to a domineering husband, finds the courage to break the engagement and marry the man she truly loves.

. . . .

lazy and inefficient; lacking ambition, initiative, or purpose.

My shiftless roommate has failed all of his classes.

SIMIAN
('sim·ee·ăn) adj.

. . . .

SINUOUS
('sin·yoo·ŭs) adj.

. . . .

SLAKE
(slayk) v.

of or like an ape or monkey.

Scientists have studied humans' simian ancestors.

. . . .

winding, undulating, serpentine.

It is dangerous to drive fast on such a sinuous road.

. . . .

1. to satisfy, quench.
2. to reduce the intensity of, moderate, allay.

The deer slaked its thirst at the river.

SODDEN
('sod·ĕn) adj.

· ·

SOLECISM
('sol·ĕ·siz·ĕm) n.

· ·

SOLICIT
(sŏ·'lis·it) v.

1. thoroughly saturated, soaked.
2. expressionless or dull, unimaginative.

Caught in an unexpected rainstorm, I was sodden by the time I reached the bus stop.

. . . .

1. a mistake in the use of language.
2. violation of good manners or etiquette, impropriety.

Frank's solecism caused his debate team much embarrassment.

. . . .

1. to ask for earnestly, to petition.
2. to seek to obtain by persuasion or formal application.
3. to approach with an offer for paid services.

Cy was touting the merits of the referendum as he solicited support for Tuesday's vote.

SOPHISTRY
('sof·i·stree) n.

. . . .

SORDID
('sor·did) adj.

. . . .

SPECIOUS
('spee·shŭs) adj.

clever but faulty reasoning; a plausible but invalid argument intended to deceive by appearing sound.

I was amused by his sophistry, but knew he had a little more research to do before he presented his argument to the distinguished scholars in his field.

. . . .

1. dirty, wretched, squalid.
2. morally degraded.

This sordid establishment should be shut down immediately.

. . . .

1. seemingly plausible but false.
2. deceptively pleasing in appearance.

Vinnie's argument was specious but untrue.

SPURIOUS
('spyoor·ee·ŭs) adj.

. . . .

SQUALID
('skwol·id) adj.

. . . .

STAUNCH
(stawnch) adj.

false, counterfeit, not genuine or authentic.

Ian's surreptitious manner makes me believe his support for you is spurious and that he has a hidden agenda.

• •

1. filthy and wretched.
2. morally repulsive, sordid.

The housing inspectors noted such deplorable and squalid living conditions in the decrepit building on Water Street that they were forced to evacuate the tenants.

• •

very devoted or loyal to a person, belief, or cause.

I have always been a staunch believer in the power of positive thinking.

STEADFAST
('sted·fast) adj.

. . . .

STOICAL
('stoh·i·kăl) adj.

. . . .

STRIDENT
('strī·děnt) adj.

S

1. firmly fixed or unchanging, resolute.
2. firmly loyal and constant, unswerving.

The captain held a steadfast course despite the rough seas.

. . . .

seemingly unaffected by pleasure or pain; indifferent, impassive.

Michael was stoical, but underneath, he is every bit as emotional as we are.

. . . .

unpleasantly loud and harsh; grating, shrill, discordant.

When he heard the strident tone of his mother's voice, Oscar knew he was in big trouble.

TOEFL iBT® VOCABULARY FLASH REVIEW

STULTIFY
('stul·tǐ·fī) v.

. . . .

STYMIE
('stī·mee) v.

. . . .

SUBLIME
(sǔ·'blīm) adj.

1. to impair or make ineffective, cripple.
2. to make (someone) look foolish or incompetent.

Of course I'm angry! You stultified me at that meeting!

. . . .

to hinder, obstruct, thwart; to prevent the accomplishment of something.

The negotiations were stymied by yet another attack.

. . . .

having noble or majestic qualities; inspiring awe, adoration, or reverence; lofty, supreme.

Beethoven's music is simply sublime.

SUBLIMINAL
(sub·ˈlim·ĭ·năl) adj.

. . . .

SUBVERT
(sub·ˈvurt) v.

. . . .

SUCCINCT
(sŭk·ˈsingkt) adj.

below the threshold of consciousness.

Subliminal advertising is devious but effective.

· ·

1. to overthrow.
2. to ruin, destroy completely.
3. to undermine.

She subverted his authority by sharing internal information with outside agents.

· ·

expressed clearly and precisely in few words; concise, terse.

Cole's eloquent and succinct essay on the power of positive thinking won first place in the essay contest.

SUCCOR
('suk·ŏr) n.

. . . .

SUNDRY
('sun·dree) adj.

. . . .

SUPERCILIOUS
(soo·pĕr·'sil·ee·ŭs) adj.

assistance or relief in time of difficulty or distress.

v. to provide assistance or relief in time of difficulty or distress.

The Red Cross and other relief organizations give succor to the needy during natural disasters.

. . . .

various, miscellaneous.

The sundry items in her backpack reveal a great deal about her personality.

. . . .

haughty, scornful, disdainful.

Sunil's supercilious attitude and sarcastic remarks annoy me greatly.

SUPPLICANT
('sup·lĭ·kănt) n.

· ·

SURFEIT
('sur·fit) n.

· ·

SURLY
('sur·lee) adj.

a person who asks humbly for something; one who beseeches or entreats.

The supplicants begged for forgiveness.

. . . .

1. an excessive amount or overabundance; glut.
2. the state of being or eating until excessively full.

v. to feed or fill to excess, satiety, or disgust; overindulge.

In some countries, the leaders and a select few enjoy a surfeit of wealth while most of the population lives in squalor.

. . . .

bad-tempered, gruff, or unfriendly in a way that suggests menace.

Emily received a surly greeting from the normally cheerful receptionist.

SURMISE
(sŭr·'mīz) v.

. . . .

SURREPTITIOUS
(sur·ĕp·'tish·ŭs) adj.

. . . .

SURROGATE
('sur·ŏ·git) n.

to infer based upon insufficient evidence; to guess, conjecture.

After finding dirty footprints in her apartment, Lakisha surmised that someone had stolen her misplaced jewelry.

. . . .

1. done, made, or obtained through stealthy, clandestine, or fraudulent means.
2. marked by or acting with stealth or secrecy.

Ian's surreptitious manner makes me believe that he has a hidden agenda.

. . . .

a substitute; one who takes the place of another.

Martha agreed to be a surrogate mother for her sister.

SVELTE
(svelt) adj.

. . . .

SYCOPHANT
('sik·ŏ·fănt) n.

. . . .

slender and graceful, suave.

The svelte actress offered a toast to her guests.

. . . .

a person who tries to win the favor of influential or powerful people through flattery; a fawning parasite.

Omar realized that one of the drawbacks of his celebrity was that he would always be surrounded by sycophants.

. . . .

TACITURN
('tas·i·turn) adj.

. . . .

TANGENTIAL
(tan·'jen·shăl) adj.

. . . .

TANGIBLE
('tan·jĭ·bĕl) adj.

habitually untalkative, reserved.

I've always known him as taciturn, but yesterday he regaled me with tales of his hiking adventures.

. . . .

1. only superficially relevant; of no substantive connection.
2. of or relating to a tangent.

Rudy's thesis paper contained only tangential statements, not relevant facts.

. . . .

able to be perceived by touch, palpable; real or concrete.

There is no tangible evidence of misconduct—it's all hearsay.

TAWDRY
('taw·dree) adj.

. . . .

TEEM
(teem) v.

. . . .

TEMERITY
(tě·'mer·i·tee) n.

gaudy or showy but without any real value; flashy and tasteless.

I've never seen such a tawdry outfit as the three-tiered taffeta prom gown that the music singer wore to the awards ceremony!

. . . .

to be full of; to be present in large numbers.

The fisherman found a stream teeming with bass.

. . . .

foolish disregard of danger; brashness, audacity.

This is no time for temerity: we must move cautiously to avoid any further damage.

TENACIOUS
(tĕ·'nay·shŭs) adj.

. . . .

TENDENTIOUS
(ten·'den·shŭs) adj.

. . . .

TENET
('ten·it) n.

1. holding firmly to something, such as a right or principle; persistent, stubbornly unyielding.
2. sticking firmly, adhesive.
3. (of memory) retentive.

When it comes to fighting for equality, she is the most tenacious person I know.

• •

biased, not impartial, partisan; supporting a particular cause or position.

The tendentious proposal caused an uproar on the U.S. Senate floor.

• •

a belief, opinion, doctrine or principle held to be true by a person, group, or organization.

This pamphlet describes the tenets of Amnesty International.

TENUOUS
('ten·yoo·ŭs) adj.

....

TERSE
(turs) adj.

....

THWART
(thwort) v.

1. unsubstantial, flimsy.
2. having little substance or validity.

Though the connection between the two crimes seemed tenuous at first, a thorough investigation showed they were committed by the same person.

. . . .

concise, using no unnecessary words, succinct.

After our disagreement, Heidi and I engaged only in terse exchanges.

. . . .

to prevent the accomplishment or realization of something.

The general thwarted an attack by the opposing army.

TIMID
('tim·id) adj.

. . . .

TIMOROUS
('tim·ŏ·rŭs) adj.

. . . .

TIRADE
('tī·rayd) n.

lacking confidence, conviction, or courage; fearful, hesitant, shy.

Adele was so timid she could barely muster the courage to look another person in the eye.

· ·

fearful, timid, afraid.

The stray dog was timorous, and it took a great deal of coaxing to get him to come near the car.

· ·

a long, angry, often highly critical speech; a violent denunciation or condemnation.

Since Andre was known for his temper, his tirade did not surprise his roommate.

TOIL
(toil) n.

. . . .

TOTALITARIAN
(toh·tal·i·'tair·ee·ăn) adj.

. . . .

TOUT
(towt) v.

exhausting labor or effort; difficult or laborious work.

v. to work laboriously, labor strenuously.

Evan toiled for hours before solving the problem.

• •

of a form of government in which those in control neither recognize nor tolerate rival parties or loyalties, demanding total submission of the individual to the needs of the state.

The totalitarian regime fell quickly when the people revolted.

• •

1. to promote or praise highly and energetically, especially with the goal of getting a customer, vote, etc.
2. to solicit (customers, votes, etc.) in an especially brazen or persistent manner.

Cy was touting the merits of the referendum as he solicited support for Tuesday's vote.

TRACTABLE
('trak·tă ·běl) adj.

. . . .

TRANSIENT
('tran·zhĕnt) adj. |

. . . .

TRENCHANT
('tren·chănt) adj.

easily managed or controlled; obedient, docile.

In the novel Brave New World, *the World Controllers use hypnosis and a "happiness drug" to make everyone tractable.*

. . . .

Lasting only a very short time; fleeting, transitory, brief.

Their relationship was transient but profound.

. . . .

1. penetrating, forceful, effective.
2. extremely perceptive, incisive.
3. clear-cut, sharply defined.

It was a trenchant argument, and it forced me to change my mind about the issue.

TRIBUNAL
(trī·'byoo·năl) n.

....

TRITE
(trīt) adj.

....

TRUCULENT
('truk·yŭ·lĕnt) adj.

a court of justice.

He will be sentenced for his war crimes by an international tribunal.

. . . .

repeated too often, overly familiar through overuse; worn out, hackneyed.

The theme of the novel was trite, as many writers had written about death in a similar way.

. . . .

1. defiantly aggressive.
2. fierce, violent.
3. bitterly expressing opposition.

The outspoken congresswoman gave a truculent speech arguing against the proposal.

TRUNCATE
('trung·kayt) v.

· ·

TUMULTUOUS
(too·'mul·choo·ŭs) adj.

· ·

TURPITUDE
('tur·pi·tood) n.

to shorten or terminate by (or as if by) cutting the top or end off.

The glitch in the software program truncated the lines of a very important document I was typing.

. . . .

1. creating an uproar; disorderly, noisy.
2. a state of confusion, turbulence, or agitation, tumult.

It was another tumultuous day for the stock market, and fluctuating prices wrought havoc for investors.

. . . .

1. wickedness.
2. a corrupt or depraved act.

Such turpitude deserves the most severe punishment.

UMBRAGE
('um·brij) n.

. . . .

UNCTUOUS
('ungk·choo·ŭs) adj.

. . . .

UNDERMINE
(un·dĕr·'mn) v.

offense, resentment.

I took great umbrage at your suggestion that I twisted the truth.

. . . .

1. unpleasantly and excessively or insincerely earnest or ingratiating.
2. containing or having the quality of oil or ointment; greasy, slippery, suave.

I left without test-driving the car because the salesperson was so unctuous that I couldn't trust him.

. . . .

1. to weaken or injure, especially by wearing away at the foundation.
2. to destroy in an underhanded way.

By telling the children that they could eat chocolate, the babysitter undermined their mother, who forbade them to eat sweets.

UNDULATE
('un·jŭ·layt) v.

. . . .

UNTOWARD
(un·'tohrd) adj.

. . . .

UPBRAID
(up·'brayd) v.

to move in waves or in a wavelike fashion, fluctuate.

The curtains undulated in the breeze.

. . . .

1. contrary to one's best interest or welfare; inconvenient, troublesome, adverse.
2. improper, unseemly, perverse.

Jackson's untoward remarks made Amelia very uncomfortable.

. . . .

to reprove, reproach sharply, condemn; admonish.

The child was upbraided for misbehaving during the ceremony.

URBANE
(ur·'bayn) adj.

. . . .

USURP
(yoo·'surp) v.

. . . .

elegant, highly refined in manners, extremely tactful and polite.

Christopher thinks he's so urbane, but he's really quite pedestrian.

. . . .

to seize, or take possession of, by force and without right; to wrongfully take over.

After the king's half-brother usurped the throne, he executed the king and queen and imprisoned the prince, who was the rightful heir to the throne.

. . . .

VACILLATE
('vas·ĭ·layt) v.

. . . .

VACUOUS
('vak·yoo·ŭs) adj.

. . . .

VEHEMENT
('vee·ĕ·mĕnt) adj.

V

1. to move or sway from side to side, fluctuate.
2. to swing back and forth about an opinion, course of action, etc.; to be indecisive, waver.

Denise vacillated for weeks before she decided to accept our offer.

. . . .

empty, purposeless; senseless, stupid, inane.

This television show is yet another vacuous sitcom.

. . . .

1. characterized by extreme intensity of emotion, forcefulness of expression, or conviction.
2. marked by great force, vigor, or energy.

The senator was vehement in her denial of any wrongdoing, and maintained her innocence throughout the investigation.

VENAL
('vee·năl) adj.

. . . .

VENERABLE
('ven·ĕ·ră·bĕl) adj.

. . . .

VERBOSE
(vĕr·'bohs) adj.

easily bribed or corrupted; unprincipled.

The venal judge was removed and disbarred.

. . . .

worthy of reverence or respect because of age, dignity, character or position.

The venerable Jimmy Carter has won the Nobel Peace Prize.

. . . .

using more words than necessary; wordy, long-winded.

Her verbose letter rambled so much that it didn't seem to have a point.

VERISIMILITUDE
(ver·i·si·'mil·i·tood) n.

. . . .

VERITABLE
('ver·i·tă ·běl) adj.

. . . .

VEX
(veks) v.

the appearance of being true or real.

*The movie aims for complete verisimilitude,
painstakingly recreating the details of everyday
life in the 1920s.*

· ·

real, true, genuine.

Einstein was a veritable genius.

· ·

1. to annoy, irritate.
2. to cause worry to.

I was completely vexed by his puerile behavior.

VIE
(vī) v.

. . . .

VIGNETTE
(vin·ˈyet) n.

. . . .

VIRULENT
(ˈvir·yŭ·lĕnt) adj.

to compete with or contend; to strive for superiority or victory.

The two scientists vied to be the first to find concrete evidence of extraterrestrial life.

• •

a brief description or depiction, especially a short literary sketch or scene or ornamental sketch in a book.

The film is a series of interrelated vignettes rather than one continuous narrative.

• •

1. extremely poisonous, injurious or infectious.
2. bitterly hostile or hateful, acrimonious.

They say that the pen is mightier than the sword; indeed, words can be every bit as virulent as the sting of a scorpion.

VIS-À-VIS
(vee·ză·'vee) adj.

. . . .

VITRIOLIC
(vit·ri·'ol·ik) adj.

. . . .

VITUPERATE
(vī·too·pĕ·rayt) v.

1. referring or directing attention to.
2. face to face with or opposite to.
adv. face to face.

After a few minutes of pandemonium, the lights came back on, and Suki suddenly found herself vis-à-vis with the man of her dreams.

· ·

savagely hostile or bitter, caustic.

Her vitriolic attack on her opponent was so hostile that it may cost her the election.

· ·

to criticize or rebuke harshly or abusively; to censure severely, berate.

After being vituperated by her boss for something that wasn't her fault, Jin handed in her letter of resignation.

VOLATILE
('vol·ă·til) adj.

. . . .

VOLUBLE
('vol·yŭ·bĕl) adj.

. . . .

VORACIOUS
(voh·'ray·shŭs) adj.

TOEFL iBT® VOCABULARY FLASH REVIEW

1. varying widely, inconstant, changeable, fickle.
2. unstable, explosive, likely to change suddenly or violently.
3. (in chemistry) evaporating readily.

The stock market has been so volatile lately that I have decided to invest in bonds instead.

. . . .

1. talking a great deal and with great ease; language marked by great fluency; rapid, nimble speech.
2. turning or rotating easily on an axis.

Your new spokesperson is very voluble, and is clearly comfortable speaking in front of large audiences.

. . . .

excessively greedy, rapacious; having a great appetite for something, devouring greedily.

I have always been a voracious reader and read dozens of books every month.

WARY
('wair·ee) adj.

. . . .

WINNOW
('win·oh) v.

. . . .

TOEFL iBT® VOCABULARY FLASH REVIEW

guarded, watchful, cautious.

After being swindled by the street vendor, Bridget was wary of most salespeople.

. . . .

1. to separate the grain from the chaff by using the wind or other current of air to blow the chaff away.
2. to separate the good from the bad; to examine or sift through to remove undesirable elements.

We have winnowed the list of applicants down to five highly qualified candidates.

. . . .

XENOPHOBIA
(zen·ŏ·ˈfoh·bee·ă) n.

. . . .

TOEFL iBT® VOCABULARY FLASH REVIEW

a strong dislike, distrust, or fear of foreigners.

Many atrocities have been committed against immigrants because of xenophobia.

. . . .

ZEALOUS
('zel·ŭs) adj.

. . . .

ZEITGEIST
('tsīt·gīst) n.

. . . .

ZENITH
('zee·nith) n.

filled with or marked by great interest or
enthusiasm; eager, earnest, fervent.

*Shalom was such a zealous student that he
begged his teacher to assign him extra
projects.*

. . . .

the spirit of the times; the general intellectual
and moral outlook or attitude characteristic of
a particular generation or period of time.

*The revolutionary zeitgeist of the 1960s and
1970s is in sharp contrast to the conservative
1950s.*

. . . .

1. the highest point, top, peak.
2. the point in the sky directly above the
observer.

*She is at the zenith of her career and has won
every case this year.*